To Alex
& Sue,
with love.

Personal Path,
Practical Feet

Jaellayna Palmer

©2017 Jaellayna Palmer

All rights reserved. No part of this publication may be reproduced, distributed, or transmitted in any form or by any means, including photocopying, recording, or other electronic or mechanical methods, without the prior written permission of the publisher, except in the case of brief quotations embodied in critical reviews.

Printed in Canada

ISBN 978-0-9958836-0-4

Jaellayna Palmer
Peace by Piece Publishing
http://www.peacebypiece-publishing.com

infopeacebypiece@gmail.com

FIN 27 09 2018

Library and Archives Canada Cataloguing in Publication

Palmer, Jaellayna, 1948-, author
        Personal path, practical feet / Jaellayna Palmer.

ISBN 978-0-9958836-0-4 (softcover)

        I. Title.

PS8631.A458P47 2017   C814'.6   C2017-903445-6

Contents

Foreword

My path as author of this book began in 2007 when I was invited to contribute to a weekly "Personal Journey" column in the Guelph Mercury (the daily newspaper in Guelph, Ontario, Canada). I never could have guessed that I was heading toward writing a full-length book. But life unfolded in its own mysterious and wondrous way, and in 2012 I met Kim Douglas in Michigan, where she was leading a writer's workshop.

Kim invited me to return a few weeks later for another workshop, this next one to be co-facilitated by Tim Moore, Manager of Bahá'í Publishing (Wilmette, IL). Midway through the several days there, Tim invited me to use those columns as the starting point (or model) for a book that he would publish. Within seconds, I agreed!

Every essay in this collection begins with an actual experience or observation from my own life. Something caught my attention, so I explored it through the lens of my understanding of the Bahá'í Writings.

The book is also enriched through anecdotes and quotations from other people, whose ideas have both inspired and informed me. Though I have no way of knowing if they would agree with how I have woven it all together, I have tried to maintain the integrity of the source materials.

After I had written an earlier draft of the completed book, Tim submitted it to the National Literature Review Committee of the Bahá'ís of the United States. I incorporated their suggestions into the manuscript, Tim sent me a publishing contract, and I eagerly signed. Ironically though, early 2016 I learned that the timing was better for me to take this on as my own project. Even with that being the case, without Tim's encouragement I would not have pursued it as far as I have.

All of the essays were reviewed by other people from diverse professional and faith backgrounds, and I am grateful for their comments that let me know where we connected in our thinking. The result is a combination of what I know, what I believe, and what I have learned. I'd like to thank Rosemary Smith, Linda Yuval, Kian Merrikh, Sandie Sparrow, Lisa Skora, Mary Nairn, Ted Smith, Lin Backer, and Pat McIntyre for their assistance in this process. I am also grateful to Jan Odell for her never-ending encouragement.

I want to offer a special thanks to Don Brown, Lisa Skora, and Kim Douglas. Without them I might not even have considered writing this book. I also want to acknowledge the participants in an online discussion forum for writers. Their enthusiasm and willingness to brainstorm titles and publishing names were instrumental to my bringing this book to its completion.

Above all, I want to thank my husband John who not only was supportive of the book but also enabled me to have the time to write it. I am blessed through his love and faith in me. And I appreciate his willingness for our real-life moments to be included in many of the essays.

Perhaps there are other people I am forgetting to list here, but that doesn't mean I am not grateful to them.

Before I close, I want to thank you — readers of this book — in joining me as I continue along my personal path with my ever-practical feet.

Note to Readers

As mentioned in the foreword, I have quoted other people throughout this book. Most will be familiar to you, some maybe not. In particular, many of the quotations are from Bahá'í sources. If you are not familiar with the Bahá'í Faith, you should probably read the short summary within the endnotes (immediately following the last essay) for a brief introduction to the sources of those quotes.

Also, I have at times used a sort of shorthand by simply saying "Writings" or "Teachings". In these instances, they refer to the body of Bahá'í Writings and not a specific source that I could have directly quoted.

Chapter 1:

Home and Garden

I. Getting at the Source

Complaining to John about my ongoing battle with weeds in the garden — they seem to be winning — I thought about how dandelions grow. If the roots aren't removed along with the leaves, stems, and flowers then the roots just get stronger.

This is parallel to a common approach to the world's problems. Addressing aboveground symptoms rather than underlying causes brings results that are both temporary and superficial. And in the meantime, the problem itself grows and even escalates.

Severe situations such as famine, epidemics, extreme weather, refuge crises, and financial failures appropriately call for immediate measures. But even while doing so, we must acknowledge that underlying issues are not being resolved. Instead we need to balance attention to urgent situations with efforts and resources aimed at fundamental causes. We must keep working toward permanent solutions — solutions that are powerful enough to affect change.

Two of our greatest challenges today are climate change and war. Neither is a new issue, and both threaten to create unalterable damage to our already beleaguered planet and its creatures, including us.

Looking first at climate change, we may be too late to avoid it, but we are not too late to slow it down and to minimize its impact. We do not have to accept environmental degradation as inevitable and unstoppable. Fortunately, despite many years of delays, we now have almost universal agreement among world leaders and scientists about the role of human activity in creating the problem. Unfortunately, even tragically, we do not have the same level of agreement about what to do and the channels through which to do the work. This means we need to be active at the level of civic engagement, and we must empower individuals to each do our part.

Considering war, some say the underlying cause is scarcity of resources and others say it is power-hungry leaders — among the many possible explanations. But surely few people truly want war, even among those who wage it. War is a desperate act, devoid of respect for others. I feel so sad when I think about the countless number of people who have never known peace.

Underpinning the world's problems is a general failure to recognize the essential unity of all people, our interdependence, and our potential. If we had a universal, collective will to clean up our mess then we could cope with climate change. And if we abandoned old prejudices and instead embraced forgiveness then we could have peace.

These words from 'Abdu'l-Bahá relate not only to these two problems but to any other we might consider:

> *Bigotry and dogmatic adherence to ancient beliefs have become the central and fundamental source of animosity among men, the obstacle to human progress, the cause of warfare and strife, the destroyer of peace, composure and welfare in the world. . . we must therefore hold fast to the tools of perception and knowledge.*[1]

What can I as an individual do every day? Beyond pulling out dandelions, what else can I remove by the root? I can be overwhelmed by the scope of problems or I can find my own way to contribute to the greater good. Fortunately, the Bahá'í Writings are rich in guidance about this very thing.

I can improve my own character and connect to my spiritual nature through prayer, reflection, and study. I can demonstrate my own freedom from prejudices, welcoming all people within my community and social spaces. I can align my beliefs with my actions through service to others. I can use my intellect to distinguish fact from dogma or superstition. I can educate myself and share what I learn about issues that have lasting importance.

At the next level of action, I can support projects and causes that can improve the welfare of the planet and its peoples. I can participate at a community level to promote principles-based governance. I can encourage others who are receptive to having a role in working toward a better future.

I recognize that weeding the garden and fixing the world are two extremes along the continuum of challenges. And yet they both begin at the same place and have the same answer. Get at the root cause and fix it — starting now.

2. Read the Instructions

The eager owner of a new techno-gizmo, I put the packaging aside and started using it. Almost immediately I was frustrated by not knowing how to turn on some of the features. And just as bad, I realized that I didn't even know what some of the features were.

Then it occurred to me to read the instructions. This may sound silly to some people, but I'm probably not the only one who doesn't begin by reading the instructions. Similarly, when I am cooking I don't follow recipes closely.

In the larger scheme of things, operating a new gadget or cooking a new dish is not important. But in some instances, instructions are important, perhaps even lifesaving. Some of the more obvious ones are traffic law, safety precautions, CPR, first aid, public health guidelines, and sanitation practices.

In our personal lives, we can seek advice and follow instructions through actions such as financial planning, education and training, career counseling, conferring with health professionals, and conducting research. And in our community, we can contribute to the greater good in countless ways.

When it comes to how to live and how to contribute to society, there are instructions for this, too. I can be guided by moral standards as well as religious teachings. As a Bahá'í I accept Bahá'u'lláh as God's most recent Manifestation. And since He affirmed the spiritual truths within other previously established religions, I am in harmony with the followers of these other Faiths.

Emphasizing the importance of religion as an organized body of thought and practice, Bahá'u'lláh stated:

Religion is the greatest of all means for the establishment of order in the world and for the peaceful contentment of all that dwell therein.[2]

During my own years as a "seeker" (yes, that's what I called myself), I was intrigued by the idea of two kinds of truths (principles): spiritual, which are unchanging; and social, which evolve and are revealed over time. The latter encompass guidance that was not present in earlier Faiths because humanity was not ready for it. Some of the key principles can be summarized as the equality of men and women; universal education; worldwide auxiliary language; standard weights and measures; elimination of extremes of wealth and poverty; spiritual solution to economic problems; authority shifted from clergy to the people; elimination of all forms of prejudice; and the agreement of science and religion. Now timely, their purpose is to create the unity of all people, and within the Bahá'í Faith I found the practical steps needed to bring them to reality, even if not within my own lifetime.

When Bahá'u'lláh first taught these principles in the mid-1800s, they were advanced for their times. But gradually these ideas are being articulated elsewhere and are gaining acceptance. One especially noteworthy example is the United Nations document titled "The Universal Declaration of Human Rights" (written in 1948). We needn't go beyond the Preamble to find statements that are consistent with the principles listed above.

Regrettably, even in the parts of the world generally labeled "developed" we fall short of fulfilling many of them. Indeed, nowhere in the world are people free from power struggles and social injustices. How much more is this the case in countries and regions where tyranny, prejudice, and injustice are the prevailing conditions? If we regard these principles as instructions for building a peaceful society, then we can work toward taking them from theory to practice.

In the words of Martin Luther King, Jr.:

Injustice anywhere is a threat to justice everywhere.[3]

So the next time I buy something, I might read the instructions first — or maybe not. What is more important though is that I follow the instructions for living a good life. Here's one instruction I can use every day: I can ask myself "What can I do today to promote unity?" And then I'll know what to do.

3. Memories from Items in My Home

Throughout my home, I have keepsakes and souvenirs collected from trips and special events. I love looking at these items and recalling the experience or location associated with them, though I admit that the details for every rock, bone, or seashell do get lost in time.

Some items don't lend themselves well to being on display on a shelf or a wall, so those are put away elsewhere — not forgotten or unappreciated, just not so visible.

This morning while looking for something else, I happened to see one of those items: a neatly folded, clean, slightly frayed hand towel. I paused, remembering how John and I had received it — an unexpected gift in Malaysia from a man whose village we had visited while on a service project. As we left via longboat, he had shyly handed it to us as a farewell gift. It might seem that a towel (and not a new one at that) is an odd gift, but we knew even at that instant that this man had few possessions. Seeing that towel this morning, I sent happy thoughts to that generous man who honored us with his generosity many years ago.

And then memories of other acts of generosity came to me. One outstanding example happened in Albania in the early 1990s, shortly after the fall of communism there. We were once again on a service project, and travel was difficult due to the country's infrastructure being a shamble. And yet every day, as we visited villages and towns (frequently arriving on foot or even by donkey) people we had never met until then offered us hospitality. Along with the overnight accommodations were meals and water, the latter being especially precious. The warmth and generosity of these people, who had suffered so much themselves, was at times overwhelming.

The people of Albania were not Bahá'ís, but the memory of their showering us with such love helps me to envision a world where strangers will be considered friends, where no one will tolerate others going hungry, and where all will be welcome. Their qualities of generosity and hospitality offer a glimpse into a more gracious future.

Shoghi Effendi wrote these words of guidance:

> . . . *to show hospitality to the stranger in our midst . . . demonstrate(s) the universality of our Teachings and the true brotherhood that animates us* . . .[4]

I also have in my house several shelves of photo albums and slides. Although I don't look at them often, I cherish the memories they chronicle — family events, beautiful scenes of nature, significant places visited. Most people don't photograph the sad, troubling and perplexing times (what would those photographs look like anyway?). So the photos bring smiles and sometimes nostalgic tears. I know people who arrived in North America as refugees, and the one thing they carried as they fled their homes were photo albums.

Whether these sorts of items are on the wall, on a shelf, or in a closet, they trigger memories. I feel connected to the people who shared the moments with me. Precious as these items are, even if I were to lose them I will not lose the gratitude I feel toward the people. And to thank them, I am inspired to be generous and hospitable to others — as they were to me.

4. What I Learned from My Hydrangea

A couple of weeks ago I noticed in our garden a hydrangea that lacked vigor, didn't seem to take nourishment, and was apparently dying. I replaced it with another plant and then, hesitant to just throw this one into the compost, tried planting it elsewhere. Much to my delight, this morning I noticed that it is flourishing, flowering, and showing signs of growth.

Again seeking parallels between natural and spiritual realities, I initially thought about how this is also the case with people. We bloom within nurturing environments. Starting with childhood, we grow best when we have a loving and stable home, good food, and both educational and enrichment opportunities.

And then I thought about this in a slightly different way. A hydrangea does not have free will, so it must have precise physical conditions in which to thrive. On the other hand, humans can choose actions and attitudes to help us adapt to wherever we happen to be.

So now I am interpreting this whole matter more expansively. I think that we also bloom when we overcome tests and difficulties, especially when we exercise our free will to go beyond our own concerns.

'Abdu'l-Bahá linked happiness with our spiritual life, and he would often greet people with the simple phrase "Be happy":

> *I tell you to be happy because we can not know the spiritual life unless we are happy!*[5]

He also wrote about the temporary state of our life circumstances:

> *Grieve thou not over the troubles and hardships of this nether world, nor be thou glad in times of ease and comfort, for both shall pass away.*[6]

These two quotations are reminders that, whether or not I am currently experiencing perfect conditions, happiness is within my mind, within my reach.

What if my spiritual side is fed through difficulties? Perhaps the people, events, and circumstances that cause the most trouble also provide an opportunity for growth. As I overcome adversity, as I remain calm and even happy, I transpose what I previously thought as good for myself with what is even better for me.

With the emphasis in the Bahá'í Faith toward social transformation, I can enlarge the scope of this idea. Frank and open consultation as the basis for cooperation is integral to translating personal growth into community growth. Together we can overcome shared adversity and improve our collective condition, and we can achieve genuine social progress. This works because we are not like plants, which rely on their environment to fulfill their requirements. We can influence — even manipulate — our environment, to shape it to our own benefit. This means that we must protect the health and vitality of the environment, too.

I just went outside again to look at the hydrangea in its new locale. The sun is shining on its brightly colored flowers. If it could talk, it might thank me for moving it to a better location. As people, we can use our free will to help everyone grow, develop, and prosper. Our happiness can come from knowing that we are moving toward creating our own human garden. That would be lovely indeed.

5. Magnetism and Attraction

I don't know how it happened, but fridge magnets have become an essential part of my kitchen. Handier than tape, they enable easy posting items such as to-do lists, phone numbers, souvenirs from recent events, and a weekly schedule of who's doing what.

Aside from their convenience, I've always been intrigued by magnets. As a child, I would put two next to each other and observe how one side attracted while the other side repelled. Later in high school chemistry class, this phenomenon was explained to me, but that didn't end my fascination with them.

The innate qualities of attraction and repulsion have parallels elsewhere in life. Beyond the obvious ways we are attracted or repelled — likes/dislikes of food, music, art, weather, etc. — what if we took this idea to a higher level? In that case attraction becomes analogous to love; repulsion is hate or enmity. Attraction is love and life; repulsion is loneliness and alienation. Attraction indicates unity; repulsion indicates disunity.

In the 13th century, Persian poet, Islamic scholar and Sufi mystic Rumi wrote about the quality of attraction among people:

We are related to one another as iron and magnet.[7]

After recognizing how attraction and magnetism are characteristic of human relations, what if we were to identify the principles of attraction and apply them in our own lives and communities? The Bahá'í Writings have frequent mention of magnetism, in both a physical and a metaphysical sense. One of my favorites by 'Abdu'l-Bahá states:

The language of kindness is the lodestone of hearts and the food of the soul.[8]

Such a simple thing: kindness. Confirmed by that quotation, I know that kindness attracts and even nourishes hearts and souls. Surely I can find opportunities to express this quality every day, encouraged by recognizing the impact it can have.

Other passages in the Writings mention service, harmony, and faith as having the power to attract heavenly strength. In practical terms, this reminds me of the effect my own acts can have, as I try to be helpful to others and to seek friendship with them. Drawing on the comparison to magnetism, the outcome will be love and unity.

During my many years as a self-employed consultant I often experienced feast or famine, i.e. I was either overwhelmed with work or worried because I wasn't. But I eventually learned that I could avoid the famine by going into motion. I consciously intensified networking, set aside more time for volunteer activities, and focussed on professional development. Time and again, in ways I never could have predicted, I would attract new business opportunities.

Much like in nature where a body in motion is known to be an attracting force, so do people become attracting when we move and grow. I am not dismissing the very real obstacles many face financially, physically, or socially; and we all have times when it seems our options are few and problems insurmountable. At those times, when we look to the community or entire world beyond our own daily lives, we might even wonder where to start.

Recognizing that we are magnetic beings gives us a starting point. The mere act of getting up, showing up, and putting out energy will attract results. It may not always be immediate or as anticipated, but we will have an effect on ourselves and others. The key idea to remember is that through motion we gain momentum and feel energized. And then that energy will be channeled through us to create a better future.

Come to think of it, maybe advice such as "get up, show up, and put out energy" should be printed onto a fridge magnet as a daily reminder.

6. Equal, Not the Same

I love mowing my lawn — seeing the green lines left by the mower, figuring out how to go around obstacles, and enjoying how good it looks when I'm done. And then, as I sweep the grass clippings off the sidewalk, I chat with my neighbors as they stroll by, with or without their dogs.

A few years ago, I took over this task from John. For awhile folks were surprised to see me doing it. They asked if John was away, was he sick, why me instead of him. Some people questioned us, claiming that I had taken over what they considered to be men's work,

This got me thinking about assumptions people make about each other, about who is suited for what, and about what is proper. Surely this is a form of prejudice.

Two of the teachings of the Bahá'í Faith are elimination of all forms of prejudice and the equality of men and women. If people were free of prejudice, there would be no reaction to a woman with a healthy husband mowing the lawn. And a true recognition of the equality of men and women would include realizing that the word "equality" does not mean "sameness." A task would simply be done by whoever is willing or available. Furthermore, sometimes the less capable person would do it in the interest of capacity building or because they wanted to. In our competitive culture, typically the so-called "best" person does a job rather than someone else who can do it well enough and is eager to contribute their time and effort.

Taking this idea to a global scale, every child should have not only adequate food and health care but also opportunities to develop their capacities. There is especially a need for girls to be educated, to enter all fields of endeavor, and to contribute to creating a future world known for vigor, cooperation, harmony, and compassion.

In the early days of the feminist movement, men were blamed for our social ills and told that they needed to change. I now think that is not enough — that a more balanced, and ultimately more successful, approach calls for personal growth of men and women alike. We share responsibility for transforming the society in which we live. The Bahá'í International Community in 1995 wrote:

> *Men must use their influence . . . to promote the systematic inclusion of women, not out of condescension or presumed self-sacrifice but out of the belief that the contributions of women are required for society to progress. Women . . . must become educated and step forward into all arenas of human activity, contributing their particular qualities, skills and experience to the social, economic and political equation. Women and men together will ensure the establishment of world peace and sustainable development of the planet.*[9]

Human society needs to move beyond cultural barriers that prevent girls and women from developing their capacities and pursuing their interests. Everyone should be free to grow and to contribute — free of others' prejudgments.

7. Home Renovation Projects

John and I are in the midst of home renovations. And even though we have had several weeks of living in a state of disarray (even total chaos), I do know that the result will look great. Fresh paint, carpets that invite barefoot walking, windows we can clearly see through, colors that match or pleasingly blend, etc. Someday it will be done and life will be normal or better again. Voilà! Transformation will have been achieved.

If only transforming one's own character were so easy! But as we all know, self-improvement is the opposite: never finished, not as predictable, and can't be subcontracted.

The Bahá'í Writings state that the purpose of life is to know and worship God, to improve one's own character, and to contribute toward the advancement of civilization. As clear as that may be, our own daily steps are not so evident.

Whatever may be a person's affiliation with a religious tradition — or through recognition of their own spiritual nature without an affiliation — it seems to begin with recognizing one's own reality. Finding myself to be essentially a spiritual being, I ponder the essence of creation, the wonders of science and nature, my relationship with other people, and my potential to impact more than my own life.

This leads into the idea of improving my own character. A person doesn't need to be a bad person to need improvement; indeed, we all need improvement. Whether we want to become more patient, generous, forgiving, grateful, curious, kind, industrious — and the list goes on — almost every day brings opportunities to learn and grow. If I consciously recognize what I want to work on, that is better yet. Much like the home renovations, I can purposely seek ways to improve. I can make a goal and take steps to practice, realizing it may be a long journey, not to be finished or just crossed off a list.

Both personal growth and social transformation are facilitated through education. This includes reading holy writings, participating in informed discussions, and other similarly purposeful endeavors — and then engaging in action. The Bahá'í International Community wrote:

> *But moral values are not mere constructs of social processes. Rather, they are expressions of the inner forces that operate in the spiritual reality of every human being, and education must concern itself with these forces if it is to tap the roots of motivation and produce meaningful and lasting change.*[10]

So how do I express these moral values? Service to others is the link between my own transformation and contributing to the advancement of civilization. Sometimes the service is organized: sorting cans and packages at the local food bank, cleaning up a park, or fundraising for a worthy cause. Often though it is subtler: helping a neighbor with chores or offering encouragement to someone who feels discouraged. I may know the other person: driving a friend to a doctor's appointment or taking care of someone's yard while they travel. Often though I may not already know the other person, as in the case of volunteering to help new immigrants with their résumés. I may offer the service as an individual. Or I may be part of a collective effort, as in the case of supporting local Bahá'í youth in their group activities.

As I go through my house now I can see progress as projects are finished. Though my own personal renovation won't be so obvious, I know that if I take the steps then it will happen. And valuable as this is, no costs will show up on my credit card statement.

8. Beautiful Things That Don't Last

Home again after a week's vacation, we eagerly went to our garden this afternoon to see what had happened while we were away. We were delighted to see new blooms on this plant, fruit starting on that tree, new seedlings taking root, and — oops, peonies come and gone. We had missed their beautiful annual display, and all that was left was a big cleanup job.

As I pruned away the deadheads and tidied up the area, I considered other beautiful things that don't last long. And about how, even though their season may be brief, they are still worthwhile.

I thought about going to a live concert, comparing that to buying a CD or downloading a song. The concert lasts only two hours, but the memory lingers. The same thing can be said about other forms of entertainment, for example stage plays compared to movies or books.

Taking this to a larger dimension, life itself is brief. Every day has beauty within it, and every experience — whether at the time it seems good or bad — holds the potential for learning and growth.

My garden has plants that I know won't last, though durations vary. Annuals will bloom for only a few days or maybe a full season; shrubs will continue for many years, maybe even decades. Trees are more enduring, living for decades or even centuries. But all are finite, mortal just like us.

My actions and achievements are limited, more like the annuals or maybe shrubs — or are they? I may think that my actions are short-lived, but it is entirely possible that little things can turn into big things and extend into the future. Here's a simple example, one that can test this idea. Suppose I clean out my closet, afterwards donating some clothes to charity. Someone in need goes to the charity's retail store, buys my skirt and blouse, wears them to a job interview, and gets the job. She does well and starts her own business. Her success and prosperity help many people. And then one day she cleans out her own closet — and so it all continues.

What about our relationships with other people? Are they time-limited? The Bahá'í Writings tell us that souls in the next world will recognize each other through a spiritual union. This will not be through vision or another means that we can understand while in this physical, temporal realm.

My own physical life is brief, but my actions can endure. I am reassured by these words from 'Abdu'l-Bahá:

> . . . life in this fast-fading world is as fleeting and inconstant as the morning wind . . . how fortunate are the great who leave a good name behind them, and the memory of a lifetime spent in the pathway of the good pleasure of God.[11]

That quotation mentions two specific qualities: a good name and a lifetime spent in the pathway of God. Along with the reassurance is a challenge and a promise. The promise is that we can be associated with worthy deeds and lofty ideals; and our actions can be indicative of a desire to serve and respect others.

If we want to leave behind a legacy of beauty, then that is what needs to be done. So simple to state, more difficult to do. Fortunately, in contrast to the short-blooming peonies, we have more than a week each year in which to try.

9. Sorting Through the Clutter

Yesterday I happened to hear a real estate broker advising someone who was preparing to sell her home. Beyond the usual items like fresh paint, clean carpets, and attractive window dressings were some recommendations that I hadn't considered — most notably the advice to reduce clutter. When she mentioned it, I thought yes, that makes sense, since visual clutter might make a prospective new owner fear that their own things wouldn't fit or would look messy. In this situation, someone might be so discouraged and distracted that they would fail to see the beauty otherwise present in the home.

This got me thinking about other forms of clutter in life. What might occupy my time and attention as it distracts me? What keeps me from accomplishing, experiencing and creating what matters the most to me? What keeps me from being immersed in beauty?

Perhaps first on the list would be worrying about the past. While we have much to learn from the past, mental clutter will result from dwelling on it, indulging in regrets, or harboring grudges. None of this is helpful, and this sort of thinking can even stand in the way of experiencing the moment and interacting with people as they presently are.

Similarly, being fretful about the future is distracting. For example, a friend told me that she's constantly making mental lists. While watching a movie she's planning her shopping; while at a concert she's rehearsing phone conversations; while walking her dog she's anticipating her next day. Though perhaps our brains can multitask, achieving balance requires presence of mind.

Being angry with others is a source of emotional clutter, too. Related to this is dwelling on the shortcomings of other people, which is one of the biggest distractions. Improving my own character and managing my own life is my responsibility, but that's where it ends. As 'Abdu'l-Bahá said:

> . . . seek out our own shortcomings before we presume to condemn the faults of others . . . we must not consider ourselves superior to our neighbours! We must be careful not to exalt ourselves lest we be humiliated.[12]

Worse yet would be allowing concern with the faults of others to lead to gossip and backbiting, as these acts are harmful to both the speaker and the listener. Bahá'u'lláh wrote:

> . . . backbiting quencheth the light of the heart, and extinguisheth the life of the soul.[13]

My spirit can be diminished and my time wasted in other ways, some of which seem normal in present Western culture. This includes being consumed in materialism, i.e. accumulating things and "living the good life," as the saying goes. The problem arises when this is carried to extremes, when attachment to the material life might overwhelm my attention to the more important work at hand — work that might even help with the advancement of society.

As New Zealand adventurer and author Barry Crump wrote:

> In the Kashmir they struggle with too little, here we struggle with too much. Half of what most of us have is twice as much as we need, and twice what they've got is half what they need.[14]

Now as I look at my schedule and my home, I am thinking more about what is essential. I want to reduce distractions, to see things more clearly, to live more simply. I want to reduce the clutter and stay on the path toward creating and living in beauty.

10. Spices: Longevity Through Variety

It's spring cleaning season, and this morning I finally got around to organizing my kitchen spice rack. While I did it, I thought about spices and how dull food would be without them.

Taking a break from my project, I decided to do some research into spices. A quotation from Hans Selye caught my eye. This notable researcher into the causes and effects of stress on animals said:

> *Variety of experience is not only the spice of life but possibly the key to longer life.*[15]

The line "variety is the spice of life" is well known, but I had thought of it in qualitative, rather than quantitative, terms. Now variety is also being associated with longevity. Science is finding that at the physiological level our brains develop and grow through exposure to new situations. Learning, problem-solving, and creative endeavors are not only pleasurable in a recreational sense but also are essential to the development of our brains. And this, researchers are telling us, can contribute to a longer life.

Though there may be other interweaving factors, it isn't hard to imagine the link from variety to brain stimulation to new brain activity to revitalized brain cells. At the same time, our sense of well-being is enhanced through variety: we grow physically stronger, we are healthier, and our enjoyment in life increases. Yes, that makes sense.

Certainly our bodies benefit from variety. We are more balanced with both upper and lower body fitness; we need both strength and stamina; athletes cross-train; we need food from all food groups; and we are told to avoid excessively repetitive movement.

There are similarities in our cultural tastes. As much as I love movies, I also read books, listen to music, and visit museums. If someone asks me what is my favorite film (or book, music, artist, etc.) I never have an answer, because my preferences and tastes change from time to time, even with the mood of the moment or in reaction to the person who happens to be asking me.

To mention the obvious, a desire for variety in food seems to be universal. Even if only the same basic foods are available, we add spices or novel ingredients for interest. I've noticed that people frequently discuss their recreational or travel plans in terms of ethnicity of food.

This line of thinking also applies to our social lives. If variety (biodiversity) is desirable in the natural world, then why not also in the social world?

'Abdu'l-Bahá suggested that we learn a lesson from nature:

> *Let us look rather at the beauty in diversity, the beauty of harmony, and learn a lesson from the vegetable creation . . . It is just the diversity and variety that constitutes its charm; each flower, each tree, each fruit, beside being beautiful in itself, brings out by contrast the qualities of the others, and shows to advantage the special loveliness of each and all.*[16]

Thinking of it in these terms, we can appreciate diversity as a source of strength rather than separation or alienation.

A workplace is enhanced through having a diverse staff, as this offers a range of perspectives that potentially bring better ideas and more effective solutions, beyond what any one person could achieve on their own. Similarly, our communities are improved when residents coming from diverse backgrounds are welcomed and even encouraged.

'Abdu'l-Bahá compared this aspect of diversity to music in saying:

> *The diversity in the human family should be the cause of love and harmony, as it is in music where many different*

notes blend together in the making of a perfect chord. If you meet those of different race and colour from yourself . . . rejoice to be among them.[17]

Whether we seek variety or it is naturally present, it brings pleasure and is mind-expanding. How wonderful now to know it can also add to my life span. Quality AND quantity of life. That is welcome news, any time of the year.

II. Planning Life, Living Life

John and I are making some important decisions — well, important to us anyway. I keep trying to think through the long-term impact, projecting events forward several years. Even as I do it, I know this is unrealistic with so many unpredictable variables ahead of us. As John Lennon famously wrote in one of his songs:

> *Life is what happens while you're busy making other plans.*[18]

Yes, there will be surprises. Some will bring better results than ever dreamed, and some will bring setbacks and delays. Possibly the plan itself will be discarded.

Confucius is said to have offered this perspective:

> *Success depends upon previous preparation, and without such preparation there is sure to be failure.*[19]

If this sort of advice seems to apply chiefly at the personal level, we might consider these words from Dwight D. Eisenhower, who was speaking from the perspective of war and national governance:

> *Plans are nothing; planning is everything.*[20]

So the point seems to be that without planning there cannot be a plan, and even a plan with limitations is better than no plan at all. The process itself challenges us to remain flexible, adapting to inevitable changes.

Regardless of the seriousness of the project being planned, the process happens in phases. It begins with having a realistic assessment of the situation. There's no point in having a plan that looks good on paper but has no chance of succeeding because it isn't grounded in reality.

Similarly, we need to know available resources. The best plan imaginable won't work without enough money to pay for it. If at this phase we discover we haven't enough funds, this may be a signal to revamp the plan or to find ways to get more money. In either case, the earlier this is known the better.

Frequently other people are involved in what we are planning. Whether they be experts with information or family members who will share in the work, having discussions with others is essential. Otherwise just one person is making assumptions, weighing options, creating lists, and possibly overlooking or misinterpreting information.

Even with these strategic steps in place, commitment and patience are essential for success. This is especially true for long-term projects, since short-term enthusiasm will not provide enough fuel to bring about results.

In our own everyday lives, we can't always do what carpenters and tailors do when they advise to "measure twice, cut once." Sometimes we just must act. If we have been planning then at least we know where we stand, even if the final plan had another timeframe or vision.

Shoghi Effendi, who was keenly skilled as a planner, often advised and encouraged the Bahá'ís of his time in their efforts to develop as a worldwide community. His many letters and books use words such as *careful planning, energetic action, great deal of patience, planning and perseverance, resolute effort* and *meticulously carried out*. Above all, and not surprisingly, he emphasized the requirements of successful planning as being:

> *Nothing short of unity, self-sacrifice and intelligent and systematized planning...*[21]

As John and I continue our conversation about our own long-term plan, we will find that the process has its own outcome, separate from the plan itself. Through planning we grow stronger and develop character traits such as patience, perseverance, detachment, and curiosity. These will see us through difficult times as well. Even if that wasn't part of the original plan.

Chapter 2:

In the Community

1. Signs and Directions to a Peaceful Destination

Living in a small town, I can easily walk to most places. While doing some errands earlier today, I noticed that the closer I got to the downtown area the more I saw signs, lots of them. Street names, stop signs, road closures, businesses open, apartments for rent, churches with special events, stores with discounts, garage sales — signs and more signs, everywhere.

And then something happened that couldn't have been better timed if it were being staged for a movie. A car pulled over, and the driver asked for help with directions. No wonder he was lost and confused, considering the barrage of signage compounded by ambiguity of some of the road names and numbers.

After helping him to get onto the right route, I considered what signs I pay attention to. With so much beckoning me in, warning me, directing me, selling to me — how do I make my own most important decisions? Beyond everyday commercial and transportation needs, what do I seek, trust, and ultimately follow? How do I navigate through this life?

As a Bahá'í I trust the teachings of Bahá'u'lláh. These teachings, which have been translated, interpreted, and implemented through His successors ('Abdu'l-Bahá, Shoghi Effendi, and the Universal House of Justice) range from the profound principle of unity to practical, world-embracing matters of governance. They emphasize elimination of all forms of prejudice, the equality of men and women, universal education, and spiritual approaches to economic problems. With these sorts of ideas guiding my actions and decisions, I can also ask myself "What would 'Abdu'l-Bahá do?" when I am uncertain or lost, perhaps even facing apparent contradictions.

Through the principle of independent investigation of the truth I am learning to discriminate between facts and propaganda; between honest reporting and bias; between integrity and commercial incentive. I do not accept everything I read or hear on the news. Instead, I consider the source and evaluate for myself as best I can. And gradually I find who I can rely on.

In the words of 'Abdu'l-Bahá:

> . . . blind imitation of the past will stunt the mind. But once every soul inquireth into truth, society will be freed from the darkness of continually repeating the past.[1]

Discussing ideas with others can be helpful. I can invite friends or other trusted people to consider difficult decisions, to help me weight options, or even just to find the right questions to ask. In true consultation, no one has a position or ego to protect. Instead of serving individual interests, we are engaged in assessing alternatives and then finding the best answer.

Yet another way to make decisions is to "follow my guts." My inner knowing is connected to personal truth in ways I can't consciously reach. If I flip a coin to choose between two options, my guts will tell me if I like the result or not. And then if I act accordingly, the relief I feel is evidence of the power of this technique.

Not all signs are visible and posted on city streets. Writing about the renewal of God's message to humanity through His own revelation, Bahá'u'lláh wrote:

> From every direction the signs have been manifested.[2]

Surely this is the case. Climate is changing, economic hardship lingering, political conflicts accelerating, and social systems deteriorating. These are signs that it is time for us to redirect our efforts and energies. If we cast aside old solutions that fail to address today's problems then we can move instead toward a global, unified approach. Then we can conduct our affairs and make decisions for the long-term benefit of all people and our planet.

These principles and practices may not help us make a choice between a left or a right turn, but they do offer guidelines for living. Carefully followed, they will someday get us to our destination: a better, more peaceful future.

2. The Benefits of City Parks

I'm not sure who was enjoying it more — the child feeding the birds or the parent watching her. Obviously the birds were happy as they gathered, hoping to catch some morsels. This scene took place in a city park, and I found it fun to watch, too.

The recreational, physical, and psychological benefits of parks are obvious: through them we preserve and connect to nature. Yet these benefits have been considered subjective, difficult if not impossible to quantify. So I'm pleased to notice a growing trend to calculate the economic value of parks and open spaces and to officially recognize them within a city's financial balance sheet.

City parks are a public trust, financed through taxes in the public interest and managed by governments or other official bodies. Admittedly it sometimes feels like we pay too many taxes, but parks are an expression of who we are as a people and what we believe to be important. If we fail to protect nature and deny access to it within our increasingly urban society, we will experience great losses, themselves beyond calculation.

I'm not an economist, and I don't claim to know how to measure all of this. But one of the motivators in finding ways to do so has been climate change. The irony is that overdevelopment and industrial practices are major contributors to the problem in the first place. We know that green spaces help the environment by improving air quality and by reducing smog and CO_2 emissions; this can be quantified. Similarly, a park's role in providing food for insects and animals can be valued in concrete terms. Improvements in human physical and mental health due to outdoor recreation and beauty can be measured. Property values in areas with parks and green spaces tend to remain stable or increase, which in turn generates tax revenue for supporting the parks.

These are among the many ways that parks and green spaces contribute to the environment and to community well-being, and they show that parks are more than just an expense. They both save and attract money, and they are investments to protect. Furthermore, a park belongs to everyone in a community and its visitors; it is an equalizer. Wealthy people readily surround themselves with beauty; parks are indifferent to a person's financial or social status.

Referring to ideas proposed by Bahá'u'lláh, the Bahá'í International Community has called for new economic models. These models will feature:

> . . . *universally agreed-upon and enforceable laws, the equitable sharing of resources, fundamental adjustments to present institutional and economic relations . . . shaped by insights that arise from a sympathetic understanding of shared experience. . .*[3]

Giving up green space is still a common practice when building a structure; and then that structure is measured through the economic activity it will generate. But finally, albeit slowly, this practice is changing. True progress, not just physical development, is indicated as economists and city authorities acknowledge the environment as a natural source of wealth. This leads to valuing it, not just trading it for something else that is more readily quantified. As such it is an example of a new economic model.

When I pass by a city park and see a child feeding birds, when I drive though eco-corridors along highways, and whenever I see open spaces I feel encouraged that our beautiful planet is being given a chance to live. Some of us cherish it without having to measure it. Others need to measure it. Either way is fine with me so long as the outcome preserves our natural environment and its treasures.

3. The Gift of Speech

The cold weather, music on the radio, ads on TV, and the chatter around me: I am surrounded by and immersed in the month of December — a season of gift giving for many people around the world. Maybe that's why I have been thinking lately about what gifts God, our Creator, has given us all.

The most obvious is the gift of life. To be here in the first place, and to have the opportunity to grow and develop through our deeds, is the greatest gift of all.

If we also have health, love, and daily purpose then we have blessings upon blessings. And if we do not, then the gift is perhaps not so apparent, and we must look harder for it.

A less obvious gift, and one that I'm thinking about now as a writer, is the gift of utterance, i.e. the ability to communicate through spoken or written words. In the calendar revealed by the Báb and then adopted by Bahá'u'lláh, "speech" is even the name of one of the 19 months, along with such other lofty concepts as knowledge, beauty, and grandeur.

I heard recently about a young man who is spending several years in a retreat in India wherein he has taken an oath of silence. I have never met this person, so I don't know his motivation or anything else about him. But as a general idea, I do question the benefit of such an extremely long-term silence and seclusion.

I recognize that personal growth can be gained through turning off the outward distractions and addressing one's own self, especially in a quiet moment. And yet, it seems to me that the purpose of this growth is to take what is learned and to use it in the real world, where we are tested by each other and where there is such a huge need for help, compassion, love, and active involvement.

Monasticism, asceticism, and long-term seclusion were not sanctioned by Bahá'u'lláh. Instead He called upon certain monks and priests to:

> . . . give up the life of seclusion and direct their steps towards the open world and busy themselves with that which will profit themselves and others.[4]

Similarly, He reminded us that practices such as sitting alone on a mountain in silent contemplation or periods of meditation should not be for an immoderate length of time and should ultimately be outward (rather than inward) focused.

We are encouraged to participate in the social realm where the application of spiritual principles and practices can make a difference. A distinction is made between being attached to the material world and being engaged in — and grateful for — its gifts. Accordingly, we are encouraged to enjoy the beauty and the comforts that are available to us.

Through the gift of utterance we can discuss, share, entertain, relate, problem-solve, reconcile, negotiate, teach, inspire, comfort, and more. With our current times calling for social salvation, and not just personal salvation, what better way than to use all the gifts that our Creator has given us.

4. A Walk Around the Neighborhood

I went for a walk this afternoon. The air was cold but the sun was bright, so I felt warmed inside. Slowing my pace, I looked around and reflected on what I observed. Many sights, both great and small, reminded me of larger truths. This didn't surprise me, as many religious traditions teach that the physical world reflects the spiritual world. As 'Abdu'l-Bahá said:

> ... the outward is the expression of the inward; the earth is the mirror of the Kingdom; the material world corresponds to the spiritual world.[5]

Most obvious was the changing of the seasons. A few flowers, still in bloom from late summer, seemed out of place. Then I thought about how plants respond at their individual pace, just as people might react differently to changes in their own environment or changes in the needs and circumstances of humankind.

Thinking further about seasons, I considered that the sequence of seasons is cyclical as well as linear. Therein is the renewal we see every spring as well as the forward movement of human enlightenment and inspiration.

I also saw evidence of competition (a plant overcrowding another), cooperation (a neighbor helping another to reroof his house), and sacrifice (a youth allowing his younger brother to win a ballgame). Competition and cooperation in nature, as in human social interactions, are common and probably speak for themselves. So while I watched the two young boys, I thought about how sacrifice is not a bad thing. To the contrary, it feels good to sacrifice for another person or for a higher cause, since the act itself is service to others and elevates the spirit.

Looking at how folks had landscaped their yards, I was attracted to gardens and areas with lots of variety. I had the same reaction to a section along the river, where the plants were wild and varied. In nature, as in people, diversity is more appealing, more magnetic, and ultimately more natural than sameness.

I then considered how tending a garden is like educating children; in both cases the goal is to bring out the highest potential of the diverse elements to promote beauty, harmony, and well-being. And just as gardens always need tending, so do people of all ages continue to need love and to grow.

After an hour or so, as the sun got lower in the sky and the air grew chilly, I realized how this reflected a spiritual truth as well. We humans are warmed in the presence of the sun. This is the case whether our bodies are being warmed by the physical sun or our spirits are being warmed by something from the nonphysical realm, such as light in the form of truth. As we turn toward it, as we let it in and illumine ourselves, we are warmed, enriched, and enlightened.

When I got home, I wondered what would happen if everyone in the neighborhood spent an hour on a similar walk. And then if afterwards we compared notes, what more might we learn — about spiritual truths and about each other.

5 Thinking About What I Don't Know

I enjoy reading the clever signs on church marquees. I recently saw one that read, "Some questions even Google can't answer." It got me thinking about different kinds of knowing. Or, as T.S. Eliot wrote:

> *Where is the wisdom we have lost in knowledge? Where is the knowledge we have lost in information?*[6]

The more easily we can look up facts the less inclined we are to dig deeply, research, reach conclusions, or develop insights — or so it seems. There is more emphasis on "what" than on "why" or "what if." I'm probably as guilty as anyone, doing an online search and quickly following a few links before moving on. I'm busy and, well, maybe that is enough.

But is it enough? It depends on what I am looking for. If it's a recipe for apple sauce, the consequence to not finding the best one is negligible. If I'm comparing prices of airline tickets, the worst case is that I might not save quite as much money as I could have.

On the other hand, in many situations precise information is essential and must not be overlooked or discarded. Without precision, where would science and math be? We need facts, and we need to have reliable ways not only to gather but also to disseminate information. This is often achieved through formal education and publishing, just to name two practical means.

Beyond information though there are other ways of knowing and understanding. As 'Abdu'l-Bahá wrote:

> *We regard knowledge and wisdom as the foundation of the progress of mankind, and extol philosophers who are endowed with broad vision.*[7]

His emphasis on broad vision tells me that I need to look beyond trivial, outward signs. Instead, if I want to grow and mature spiritually then I need to look under the surface and to seek inner meaning. I must learn to recognize the distinctions among information, knowledge, and wisdom. This will require my devoting both time and energy to reach higher levels.

Moving from information to the next level (becoming knowledgeable) is both intellectually satisfying and empowering. Shifting from information seeking to knowledge generation entails such tasks as investigating closely, exercising critical judgment while searching through evidence, and putting to use what has been learned. In its full application, this shift is in the realm of innovation and invention, and it inspires creativity.

As challenging as that can be, acquiring wisdom is the next higher level. In seeking wisdom we choose among possibly conflicting options, consider long-term impacts, resolve ambiguity, weigh the interplay of mercy and justice, and deal with other intangible concepts. There is no limit to how wise we can become, and the pursuit itself can take a lifetime.

How do we achieve wisdom and what do we do with it? Often it is a solitary experience, as we think reflectively. Sometimes it is active, as we share insights with others. And yet other times it is social, as in the process of consultation wherein we discuss a question with others who have a sincere interest in the outcome and who value truth over ego.

All of this suggests that acquiring wisdom requires patience, courage, and trust in both ourselves and others. Eventually these qualities also bring spiritual, intellectual, and emotional maturity. Perhaps this is why wisdom is so often associated with older persons.

A personal goal is therefore not only to live long but also to attain wisdom along the way. It may also be yet one more reason to spend less time at the computer — including Google searches — and more time engaging in the real world with real people.

6. Protective Gear for Body and Soul

This morning I was getting ready to bicycle to some local shops. As I put on my helmet and checked that I also had my lock and key, I thought about other forms of protective gear, other ways I protect my body and my possessions. When I drive my car, I secure my seat belt around my waist and shoulder. When I leave my house, I turn off lights and then lock the door. When I go to the beach, I take a hat and sunscreen. I do a backup of my computer every few weeks. And so on.

And then I wondered: How do I protect my self — that part of me that defines who I am and that is essential to my existence? Since I have a spiritual nature as well as a physical body, what are my risks and what do I do about them?

As a Bahá'í I am guided by the teachings of Bahá'u'lláh. This source of faith and trust helps me interpret and cope with troubles. Rather than being depressed by the morning news each day, I can envision where these times are taking us. This helps me to orient my own actions toward solutions.

Prayer, contemplation, and study as part of each day offer protection — similar to what daily physical exercise does for my body. Connecting with my higher nature and contemplating truth helps to restore balance and protects me from being mired in confusion and negativity.

We are surrounded by negativity, so vigilance is required. Sometimes it's hard to avoid, for example at a workplace where complaining and gossip are part of the daily culture. I can try to turn the conversation toward other directions or to leave the room. If I do this consistently then I am helping to protect my colleagues, too.

Whether or not I have a workplace, having daily purpose protects me from idleness and boredom. This may be a place to go, a task to do, or people to see. Whatever may be the specifics, the point is to have something that offers satisfaction and makes the day worthwhile.

Offering help to others is beneficial for them as well as a protection for me. It shifts the focus from my own needs to the needs of others, thus protecting me from becoming overly self-indulgent. Group projects have the added advantage of bringing together like-minded people, which elevates the spirit and prevents feelings of isolation.

Trusting my friends and offering mutual support is a protection from becoming self-absorbed. Rather than dwelling on my own troubles, I am genuinely concerned for others in an ongoing relationship.

Obviously not all relationships are alike and not every encounter is the same, but some of my favorite times are when we laugh together. The well-known phrase "Laughter is the best medicine" has its origins in the Bible:

A cheerful heart is good medicine.[8]

Most of us have had the experience of feeling better after a hearty laugh, and science has investigated the reason for this. The first book I ever read by a Bahá'í (William Sears) is called *God Loves Laughter*[9]. Reading it while experiencing tremendous personal difficulties, I was helped along my own path by the author's humor and refreshing honesty.

A bike helmet does not guarantee I won't fall; nothing can guarantee no mishaps to our bodies and possessions. On the other hand, protection for the inner self ultimately comes from what we do and not just what we say, especially if what we do has been guided by principles that elevate us. Living as best we can with consideration for others is the best protection for what truly matters.

7. Gratitude for Farmers

John and I went to a large agricultural fair this weekend. We had a great time visiting traditional exhibits of vintage farm machinery and hand tools. We watched a rodeo, a lumberjack competition, and barn raising. We even saw square dancing tractors. (Yes, there is such a thing.) Maneuvered through actual square dance patterns with a live caller, those tractors seemed almost as nimble as human dancers. The costumed drivers looked joyful even as they concentrated on operating machinery in such an unusual, at times even dangerous, way — to the delight of the crowd.

Looking around the large audience, I saw a wide spectrum of people including city and country folks, older people possibly reliving their own roots, and busloads of school children on an outing. I think the reason for the broad range of visitors is a universal connection to our planet and each other through farming. Taking a day to celebrate agriculture is enriching, educational, and entertaining.

In the Bahá'í Faith, the role of the farmer is a lofty one. We are grateful for the labor that raises our food, and we acknowledge the farmer's role in both local and worldwide economics. As 'Abdu'l-Bahá wrote in discussing a future system for economics:

> . . . we must begin with the farmer; there will we lay a foundation for system and order because the peasant class and the agricultural class exceed other classes in the importance of their service.[10]

To learn more about farmers today, I did some research and was particularly impressed by this statement on Greenpeace's website:

Agriculture is by far the biggest business of the world. It is estimated that 2.6 billion people or 40 percent of the world's population are small farmers. The large majority of them cultivate less than five acres of land. Small-scale farmers form the larger part of global agricultural land, produce most of the global food and at the same time host the majority of poor and hungry worldwide.[11]

As I reflected on this, I wondered especially about small farmers and their daily lives. Does our public policy give priority to improving farm methods and distribution systems, ensuring food security, and raising the living standards of farmers? What about my own actions as an individual consumer? I do try to support local farmers and seek Fair Trade for items that are not locally grown or processed. Beyond that, I can add my voice to the larger public concern in defense of farmers and farm laborers everywhere. These are complex issues, and answers will materialize as we further integrate the principle of justice into our society and our world.

The agricultural fair, representing both large and small farming, was the convergence of traditional practices and contemporary issues. This was accomplished through many exhibits with themes such as rain water harvesting, sustainable agricultural practices, backyard and patio farming ideas, organic gardening, responsible trail habits, and eco-friendly commercial products. I noticed school groups paying close attention to these exhibits. Even if most of the children will not be farmers, they will have opportunities to implement these ideas in other ways.

Though I was raised as a city girl, I've been to many county and state fairs over the years. Each time I learn something new and am reminded of the importance of farmers. This may sound obvious, but in a frequently busy and increasingly commercial urban environment, it is good to be reminded about the foundations for agriculture laid by previous generations.

As we drove home, I recalled the advice "If a farmer didn't grow it, don't eat it." Looking forward to my supper of fresh foods, the words that went through my mind were "Thank you, Farmers."

8. Happy Whatever-This-Month-Is-To-You

Every day is a special day to someone-somewhere: a birthday, an anniversary, or perhaps a long-awaited event. On a larger scale, there are civic holidays, religious holy days, and cultural celebrations. With so many occasions on a collective level, it is impractical to know what they all are, much less to observe them.

So I have been trying to learn about special *months* rather than special *days*. Checking to see what significance the current month of April may have, I discovered that it is broadly observed as Multicultural Communications Month. Even as I admire that name and salute the concept, I am thinking that the phrase is not completely clear to me.

Though the purpose is to bring us together, the word "multicultural" seems to focus on our differences more than what we have in common, which is that we all belong to the human family. And if we were to look at our differences — or distinctions — we would need to go beyond cultural; they also embrace religious, socioeconomic, racial, and other human characteristics.

Even if I cannot completely reconcile the definition of multicultural, as a Bahá'í I support actions whose purpose is to promote peace based on respect for human rights and diversity. And though the following words of Bahá'u'lláh are specifically about religion, we might generalize them to refer to a range of human diversity:

> *Consort with the followers of all religions in a spirit of friendliness and fellowship.*[12]

This idea links to my conviction that a peaceful society is strengthened by the diversity of its members; that it progresses through individuals' independent search for truth; and that it is ordered by laws which protect the rights of all people regardless of their physical characteristics, their religious beliefs, their national heritage, or their social practices.

I also think that the larger concept of freedom — including the freedoms of religion, belief, and cultural expression — is enhanced by exposure to new ideas and the ability to share and receive information. This is where the communication part of the phrase "multicultural communication" plays its part.

The word "communications" has at least two distinct instances. It can refer to one-way broadcasting (not as personal but nevertheless effective) as well as two-way conversation (between friends or among groups).

The first aspect of communications (one-way broadcasting) is served through mass media channels such as newspapers, magazines, websites, and educational materials. Taking the initiative to learn on my own is both intellectually satisfying and within my own control. In many situations though, more can be learned through social engagement such as conversation.

In a tolerant world, we would not have so much emphasis on where a person is from or what their ancestors did or did not do. Instead, we would assume that everyone has a story and we would enjoy learning about it. We would not think we had to take steps to build bridges or mend hurt feelings. Rather we would take for granted that the one thing we all have in common is that we are all uniquely different.

In the meantime, the conscious effort to reach out is important. And it is a well-spent month if within it we encourage people to appreciate each other.

9. As We Develop, Do We Also Progress?

It doesn't seem to matter whether I am listening to the car radio, streaming news on my tablet, watching a current affairs program on TV, reading online newspapers, skimming journals and blogs — a topic of ongoing interest is economic growth, or the lack of it. There are reports about advances in innovation, or the lack of it. And in areas of general interest such as arts and sports, there are reports about the number of awards or trophies won, or not.

In general, we pay attention to these sorts of quantifiable items. And although they are significant, I wonder about other elements of life that, though difficult to measure, have as great or even greater impact on our well-being. This is true whether we are considering our own local communities or the world-at-large.

As a society, are we better or worse off? What are the metrics for human health and well-being, family cohesiveness, happiness, and optimism? Are we reducing racism and other forms of prejudice? What about access to education? Are people finding their jobs meaningful? Even if most people are doing well, what about those who are not?

At the global level, what about planetary health, collective and individual security, cross-cultural communications, citizen engagement, and individual empowerment? Are there substantial advances toward the equality of men and women? What about child soldiers and sex slaves?

Various agencies and institutions around the globe report on some of these items, despite their being so difficult to measure with precision. For example, just to name some of the major successes in health and sanitation issues: polio is almost eradicated in most of the world; water purification projects are underway in Bangladesh and elsewhere; the number of new smokers has decreased; and advances in medicine have led to a decrease in war casualties. I am encouraged when I learn about these sorts of things, as they indicate one aspect of progress.

If we could ask the animals, what would they say? What about air, water, soil, and plants? What worries parents about their children's future? Are our communities becoming more or less attractive, litter-free, and well-tended?

These words from Bahá'u'lláh set a high standard:

> *Let each morn be better than its eve and each morrow richer than its yesterday.*[13]

How will I know if things are better and richer than previously? And what can I do to contribute to true progress?

Most of us are busy people, and we cannot have a large impact on our community, much less other cities, countries or the entire planet. I don't have visions of grandiosity, thinking I can single-handedly take on the big issues. On the other hand, I can orient my own actions toward love and friendship. As advised by 'Abdu'l-Bahá:

> *. . . spiritual and material developments are conditioned upon love and amity among all men.*[14]

With this in mind, I can direct my thoughts to higher ideals and let those guide my behavior and influence my communications. I can be a good listener, sincerely seeking input from others. I can be deliberate in my buying habits, patronizing stores and businesses whose standards are consistent with mine. I can support community leaders whose vision mirrors mine. I can donate money or time to worthy causes.

If I orient myself toward the outer world rather than myself, then my thoughts and actions will be ennobled. Bahá'u'lláh advised:

> *Let your vision be world-embracing, rather than confined to your own self.*[15]

I can follow the specific guidance offered through His teachings. I can seek justice, confirming that my motives are correctly aligned. I can be grateful, sharing my good fortune. I can be mindful of the spiritual nature of life, seeking to learn and be inspired by daily events.

Keeping in mind what this is all about — the community and not just me — will contribute to true progress and not just material development. If we all did that all the time, that would indeed be news.

10. Justice: It's Not Just-Us

I have been asked by a group within my community to give a talk about social justice. Through researching and thinking about this concept, I have concluded that there cannot be *justice* until people realize that there's more than *just-us* out there.

Okay, I know that's a play on words, but I do think that the truth is within the similar-sounding words in our language. What if we made our decisions, planned our policies, governed ourselves, and managed resources with the guiding principle being that it's not *just-us*?

The unity of humanity is one of the fundaments teachings in the Bahá'í Faith, so now I'm thinking about how this relates to justice. If we were to value the essential oneness of all people rather than emphasize superficial differences, suitable actions can become apparent and justice can be achieved.

In decision making and policy planning, persons in a position of influence and power need to consider that it's not *just-us*. I must not take for granted my own relatively comfortable life nor overlook the injustices that surround me. To the contrary, as an individual and as a member of organizations and institutions that operate within this society, I want to be increasingly cognizant of minorities and others who might otherwise be disenfranchised. The question "Who is missing from the conference table" would prompt a reminder to include them, too. And possibly they deserve disproportionately more consideration, since exercising justice can also be a means to eliminate the extremes of poverty and wealth.

Meeting material needs, providing universal access to education, aligning every level of our society to promote economic and social justice — these are essential elements, though they are not sufficient unless public will, as articulated through its governance, is in accord.

Thinking now about governance, I have observed countless times that divisive, partisan politics work against rather than for justice. The Bahá'í International Community has described an alternative approach and what it can achieve:

> ...a world federal system, guided by universally agreed upon and enforceable laws, will allow nation states to manage cooperatively an increasingly interdependent and rapidly changing world, thereby ensuring peace and social and economic justice for all the world's peoples.[16]

If such a system can bring social and economic justice for all, then the time and effort required to create it will be worthwhile.

Considering next the earth's natural resources, surely they do not belong to people who just happen to be born nearby, nor do they belong to people who have the financial muscle to exploit and control them. Both extremes are a *just-us* approach. On the other hand, through applying the principle of justice we would manage resources globally with a view toward long-term sustainability and equitable distribution. Moving from the notion of ownership to that of stewardship, we would protect resources in the interest of all peoples and not hold anyone hostage to short-sighted politics and private financial interests.

Until both the material and the spiritual needs and aspirations of individuals are acknowledged, development efforts will largely continue to fail. Human happiness, security, social cohesion, and economic justice are not by-products of material success. Rather, they result from complex and dynamic interactions among the satisfaction of physical requirements, social needs, and the spiritual fulfillment of the individual.

'Abdu'l-Bahá promised:

> ...justice will become manifest in human conditions and affairs, and all mankind will find comfort and enjoyment in life.[17]

With this assurance that the future will be just, the challenge is to get from here to there. To fulfill this vision for a unified and peaceful world, ideally everyone will contribute. Not just us.

II. With Thanks — Now and Always

Even with phrases such as "be here now" reminding me to slow down and to be attentive to the present, I sometimes get distracted by other things. I was thinking about this today as I looked at my to-do list. That's when I also realized that the word "now" does not always refer to an instant of time but might instead refer to a season or a trend which I am experiencing. Right now in North America, we are in the season of Thanksgiving. And though the specific holiday we call Thanksgiving is not celebrated everywhere, the practice of celebrating harvest and abundance is almost universal. This is a time of gratitude, happiness, and sharing.

'Abdu'l-Bahá emphasized being happy in all seasons, all times:

> *If we are not happy and joyous at this season, for what other season shall we wait and for what other time shall we look?*[18]

If I am not happy now, if I am not content now, then I have missed the point — which is that my life is full of blessings and that my circumstances need not define my attitude. I cannot always control what happens to me, but I can control my reaction to it.

Without trivializing or disregarding the depth and breadth of either the world's problems or the concerns in any individual's life, I am thinking now about items that sometimes seem to occupy too much time and attention.

Hopelessly behind in my reading as well as a huge backlog of emails to answer and letters to write? At least I can read and write. Here in North America, 7% of the people are functionally illiterate.

Groceries are getting low and I haven't time to go shopping, plus food prices have gone up? Almost 9% of the entire human population is said to be malnourished; and in many places the figure is well over 50%.

My car needs body work and my commute to work is getting tedious? Only about 10% of the world's people even own a car. And many millions of people walk long distances, just to get water for their families.

Noisy kids playing in my neighbor's yard? These are happy sounds. What if I were hearing gunshots or bombs instead?

House messy with projects that I don't have time for due to my job? And is that job feeling stressful? With unemployment an ongoing concern in much of the world, I am fortunate to have a job. And even better, it allows me vacation leave. And yes, the laundry will get done, too.

Deadline upon me for one of my writing projects? I am fortunate to live in a country where freedom of speech is guaranteed, even encouraged. It's hard to imagine living without newspapers, magazines, freedom of the press, or open dialogue — and instead to be repressed and censored. And yet that is reality for much of the world.

I am fortunate. With such a stable foundation from which to live, I am better able to deal with the more serious matters in my life. And most importantly, I can give time and attention to the larger world. As I do this, I am thankful for the many blessings in my life. Here and now.

Chapter 3

On the Job

I. Thoughts During My Morning Commute

I like to ask people what they do to pass time during their daily commute — whether that be by car, bus, train, bicycle, or foot. My own career has had me alternate between being home-based, going to an out-of-town workplace, or being on-site with clients. Since none of these offer me a chance to read or chat with strangers, I have found other ways to stay amused. Fortunately, I enjoy listening to the radio: news in the morning and then music (especially oldies) on the way home. And as I drive through a town, I look at signs to get a sense of what's going on locally. Sometimes I am treated to an especially witty or insightful church marquee, for example this one from a few years ago:

Whatever you are, be a good one.[1]

My initial reaction was that this uplifting advice would guide us to being better people. And then, as I thought about it further, I explored some nuances within it.

The "whatever you are" suggests that my job is equivalent to my identity. People say "I am a lawyer/teacher/chef/plumber" as if their occupation defines them. And while it is true that our jobs reflect who we are and how we spend much of our time, surely there is more to it.

From a Bahá'í perspective, my work as a person — developing my character and contributing to society — is distinct from my occupation or job. As such, work can also encompass personal interests and hobbies. For example, John, whose job is in a technical field, applies his attention to detail to at-home projects. The past several weeks he has been doing stonework in our backyard, carefully shaping and smoothing the stones. When I watch him doing this, I might see it in its nobler context: striving for excellence.

'Abdu'l-Bahá encouraged excellence in arts, crafts, and sciences. Telling us that they have a role in uplifting humanity, he said:

> *Arts, sciences and all crafts are worship . . . all effort and exertion put forth by man from the fullness of his heart is worship, if it is prompted by the highest motives and the will to do service to humanity.*[2]

Continuing my reflection on the church marquee's statement, what about the word "good"? Yes, we should be good, though I wonder what the standard is. Some jobs have external standards, such as doing so-many actions in so-many hours. Frequently though, words like "good" are more vaguely or intangibly used in the workplace. And anyway, isn't it preferable to go beyond the minimum expectation? Athletes do this, with their goal being to exceed their own personal best.

When I go to my job, I try to be at my best in order to do my best. Admittedly some days and some tasks are more motivating than others, but my work deserves my giving it all, and that will be reflected in what I do in my occupation. So if my job is one of the ways that my own inner work takes place, then the challenges it presents take on an enlarged meaning. I can learn to welcome these challenges as an opportunity to become more than good: to achieve my own personal best.

2. Coffee and Kindness to All

When I tried to pay for my coffee this morning, I was told it had already been paid for. The cashier then pointed to a woman near the exit and said that she sometimes buys coffee for strangers. Wow — I was the recipient of a random act of kindness! Catching up with her, I thanked her and told her that she had not only given me a pleasurable surprise but also had inspired me to do the same for someone else. We might call this "pay it forward." She hadn't expected to be identified and thanked personally; she had done it for the joy of giving.

This incident is a perfect example of the old saying "It's the little things in life that count." Reflecting on it, I think her actions indicate belief in the future and the role we can all play in it. My life wasn't changed by a free cup of coffee, but being at the receiving end of a stranger's kindness — yes, that is life-affirming. And because it brought me pleasure, I want to do it for others. It also has me thinking about my relationship with strangers.

'Abdu'l-Bahá wrote:

> *See ye no strangers; rather see all men as friends, for love and unity come hard when ye fix your gaze on otherness.*[3]

These words are also a reminder that we can transform the stranger into a friend and an enemy into a true brother. It tells me that if I recognize the intrinsic goodness in others then I will want to be kind, respectful, and generous to them.

Being the random recipient of a free cup of coffee has yet another aspect to it. My benefactor had no way of knowing in advance who would get the coffee and whether that person would be worthy of it. Her assumption seemed to be that anyone and everyone is worthy. So the point isn't about the coffee as much as about the anonymous, gracious nature of the act itself.

One of the fundamental teachings of the Bahá'í Faith is fellowship with stranger and friend alike. This means not only being considerate and kind but also trusting that others deserve respect and love. So many of the world's problems are caused by long-standing grudges, senseless quarrels, and entrenched animosity. Loving acts, both great and small, help to counter this.

What is required to make change? 'Abdu'l-Bahá told us what is required:

> . . . a power above and beyond the powers of nature must needs be brought to bear, to change this black darkness into light, and these hatreds and resentments, grudges and spites, these endless wrangles and wars, into fellowship and love amongst all the peoples of the earth. This power is none other than the breathings of the Holy Spirit and the mighty inflow of the Word of God.[4]

I realize that lofty words and ideas alone do not promise an immediate transformation and that a small gesture such as a cup of coffee is not enough to bring about forgiveness, universal love, or world peace. But it was an uplifting start to my work day.

3. When a Workplace Lacks Vision

With recent changes in my job situation, I am reflecting on the various places I've worked over the years, including organizations I used to visit as an outside consultant.

I've noticed that one of the biggest obstacles to productivity is low morale; and the biggest contributor to this is lack of vision. "Disunity" is another way to state this.

A workplace without a clear vision of either its purpose or its operating principles is like a car without steering or braking. No matter how powerful it may be, it isn't going anywhere, at least not intentionally. It is more likely to crash than to stall.

An organization — whether a business, a charity, a service or social club, or any other type of group venture — has an imperative to align its operations with its vision and purpose. Lacking that, disunity will result. This is true even if the individuals are well-intentioned. Disunity also invites private agendas to be pursued; in this case, contradictory interpretations can prevail and conflicts may arise. People lose trust in each other, and backbiting and gossip start to occur more frequently.

Tempted as we might be to point blame, I think it is everyone's problem — in the sense that everyone is affected by it. In times of high unemployment, many are happy to have work, even unsatisfactory work; I recognize and respect that. But wouldn't it be even better to feel inspired by one's job, to be proud of the organization, to feel part of its good work or products?

In most organizations, senior managers have the authority to initiate improvement and change. But even if they are empowered to do so, they will not be effective unless they themselves know where they want to go and have the means to communicate it. This in turn requires a vision for the future; honest, open communications; purposeful, structured mechanisms for input; a spirit of cooperation and collaboration; and recognition of the worthiness and nobility of all people. Lacking that, employees and associates will likely feel manipulated, resentful, and frustrated by the resulting disorganization.

Bahá'u'lláh taught that humanity is ready for unity, and we are collectively mature enough to achieve it. He didn't say that it will be immediate, but He reassured us that it is inevitable and provided the tools to bring it to reality.

The Universal House of Justice brought this to a practical, daily level in writing:

> . . . *these other ills are but various symptoms and side effects of the basic disease — disunity . . . It permeates attitudes in all departments of life. It is at the heart of all major conflicts between nations and peoples.*[5]

Unity. Sometimes it seems so far away and unattainable. But it must begin somewhere. As an individual, I can begin with the people I am in contact with – including family, friends, neighbors, and colleagues. If I respect them, I will communicate honestly and lovingly. I will be open-minded and free from prejudice. All people who envision a peaceful future when unity will prevail can take us closer to a loftier vision for our workplaces. That is indeed a worthy and necessary goal.

4. Living a Two-List Life

A colleague sent me an email today lamenting, "I have two lists — one immediate (which grows ever longer) and the regular list which stays the same."

I enjoyed his wit and also felt sympathetic. Yes, it does seem like there are always things to do, even while new immediate items keep popping up. As a consequence, the regular list just seems to languish. The resulting tussle between the two contributes to the breathless, stressful, even anxious state in which many of us find ourselves.

Journalist and humorist H. Allen Smith had a fun way of explaining lists:

> *The human animal differs from the lesser primates in his passion for lists.*[6]

I admit that I do like lists. They make me feel more in control, both on the job and at home. So this evening, intrigued with my colleague's comments, I tried sorting mine into two lists depending on whether the items seemed to be immediate or regular.

I noticed that some items had been there for a long time. If this was because they no longer have meaning, I took a deep breath then deleted them. Next I looked at what was left and sorted them into one list or the other.

I decided that "immediate" meant anything with high impact outcomes for either myself or others. Two other criteria were whether delaying would make them more difficult to do or if they had an actual deadline imposed by others.

Everything else went onto the "regular" list, but that didn't mean they weren't worthwhile. I realized that if I don't make a point of getting to them then they will probably never get done. I must take time for myself and sometimes be willing to do regular tasks, temporarily postponing the otherwise immediate ones. Whether this is planning for an event, taking steps toward a vacation, sorting through a stack of papers, or anything else that seems like it could be put off — they belong to a scheduled time.

Dan Millman, athlete, author, and pioneer in the self-help field, said:

> *I learned that we can do anything, but we can't do everything . . . at least not at the same time. So think of your priorities not in terms of what activities you do, but when you do them. Timing is everything.*[7]

I have a friend who schedules for herself a power hour for tasks that otherwise won't get tended to. I like this idea, as I am motivated by making progress and building momentum. If I can't actually finish the task within the hour, I have the option of continuing or not. Hopefully I can develop the insight to recognize interim steps and have confidence in long-term results.

In the words of 'Abdu'l-Bahá, speaking about items greater than my own to-do lists:

> *Knowledge is the first step; resolve, the second step; action, its fulfillment, is the third step.*[8]

Just putting something on the list is a start. But resolve requires more passion, commitment, and energy. Scheduling, follow-up, and concrete steps are indicative of action. Fulfillment — being able to cross something off of the list as finished — brings satisfaction.

Several years ago I attended a lecture on setting goals. The speaker suggested putting an item on our list that we're going to do anyway, to guarantee having something to mark as finished later. I'm not keen on trying to fool myself to that extent. Instead I want to learn to juggle better, to keep immediate items in perspective, and to pay attention to the regular items. My goal is to someday return to having just one list again and not feel overwhelmed by it. Maybe I should put THAT on my list, too.

5. Group Work on the Job

I left my iPod at home this morning, so as an alternative I went to a website that streams oldies. When I heard one of the many recorded versions of the song "No Man Is an Island," I remembered singing it at summer camp as a kid. Before this morning, I hadn't heard it for many years, but the words are as true today as when John Donne wrote the poem in 1624.[9]

Incorporated into every workplace is the need to communicate and the need to cooperate. In recent years though, the ways we do this have changed. No longer are memos and meetings the norm. Instead, people email each other, even when sitting in the same room. Texting has replaced or supplements the proverbial water cooler. Power lunches of the 80s are now just as likely to be done via real-time software. Detailed reports may be reduced to bullet lists. And rather than focusing on issues we are just as likely to be multitasking.

With so many options, the means for communications may be convenient. But what about the quality of the output? Has convenience replaced intimacy? Are we listening to each other? Is there true consultation, i.e. a concerted effort to find the truth and to reach consensus?

Emails, texting, and bullet lists are sufficient for transmitting information and are especially effective for announcing news or broadcasting updates. But when there are problems to solve, decisions to make, or issues to face then I prefer to sit down with others in real-time, without distractions; and we can use our technology to include persons who would otherwise miss the meeting.

When we are together, how do we work together? I once went to a retreat that turned out to be just senior management making announcements.

And countless times I have been at so-called "consultations" that were just opposing sides arguing for adoption of their agenda.

But there have been other times, precious and uplifting times, when true consultation has occurred. They haven't only been Bahá'í gatherings, though they did follow the Bahá'í concept of consultation. This has several aspects to it that are not present in most group meetings or events.

The process begins with fact-finding rather than with the presentation and defense of opposing positions. All ideas belong to the group, no longer associated with the person who originated them. This serves to separate personalities from the issues. Following a frank and open discussion, the group tries to reach a unanimous decision, but if that cannot be achieved then the majority vote will prevail. And as soon as the decision is made then everyone, even the previous minority, supports the group decision.

The result of this process is unity of vision and unity in action; everyone is now moving in the same direction rather than trying to subvert others. This approach to consultation puts the interest of the whole ahead of individual or partisan interests. And since everyone has had a chance to participate and to voice their concerns, no one has been marginalized.

I realize this sounds idealistic. And to anyone who hasn't experienced it themselves, it might even seem impractical. That doesn't surprise me, because it poses several challenges.

Firstly, it requires detachment. Often the decisions do not turn out as expected. Lacking detachment, we go to meetings armed with determination (maybe even a mandate) to sell our ideas and to convince others. Through consultation though, we can channel the passion behind those feelings into a search for truth or the best way. When this happens, we have become detached.

Secondly, it requires letting go of notions of power or ego. Taking its place is teamwork and group solidarity. Again, this isn't easy, especially because it requires trust in others' good intentions. One of the things we need to realize is that if we all work in the same direction then we can evaluate the worthiness of our decisions and, if necessary, tweak or rethink without anyone assigning blame to anyone else.

In many, maybe even most, workplaces these ideas will take time to achieve. So group members might be motivated by considering the impact that consultation can have on their own personal growth. As the Bahá'í International Community wrote in its paper titled "Women and Development":

> *The consultative process itself promotes personal growth and collective solidarity.*[10]

Tempted as I might be to work alone, that's not where my potential is fulfilled. Nor is it where the best results will be found. As the song said: "No Man Is an Island." Not even me.

6. Smile or Frown: Pass It On

The friendly woman at a checkout counter this morning recognized me from the photo on my newspaper column. And then she told me that she routinely posts the columns on the bulletin board in her workplace's employee lounge. I felt flattered and appreciative, to say the least. When I mentioned that I was trying to come up with an idea for my next column, she suggested, with a teasing nod toward one of her colleagues, "How about working with difficult people?" The other person's good-natured retort was "Yes, but which of us is the difficult person?" The three of us shared a laugh at this.

Now that I am back in my own office I am thinking about what makes a person difficult to work with. I once worked with someone who got increasingly negative as others around her got positive, apparently thinking this proved that she had it worse than the rest of us and then wearing that as a badge of honor. This created a tense, even toxic, atmosphere at work.

Another common experience is having a negative reaction to an ungrateful person, a demeaning joke, or a hurtful act. The reverse is also true, for example a positive reaction to an unexpected smile, a good deed, or an upbeat story. Some people tend to bring us down, while others make us feel good — why?

'Abdu'l-Bahá said:

> . . . as diseases in the world of bodies are extremely contagious, so, in the same way, qualities of spirit and heart are extremely contagious . . . both health and sickness are contagious.[11]

When I think about the people in my life, both past and present, I realize that those who made me feel good didn't do so because their lives were perfect but because they had a healthy attitude and their focus was outward, not inward. Even when they had difficulties they did not dwell on the negative, and they never tried to drag others down with them.

Close friends see each other in the best and the worst of times, and not every day will be a happy one. When we have such friends we are fortunate, and we can share cheerful times as well as grumpy moments. That's part of being honest with each other.

But in the workplace or other public spaces, especially anywhere that relationships are based on proximity, we serve best by finding ways to uplift each other. In these cases, if I can focus on the fullness of my life and be confident about the positive effect one person can have on another, then I can fulfill this phrase from Bahá'u'lláh:

(L)ook upon him with a bright and friendly face.[12]

Since both wellness and disease can be contagious, my hope is that I can be the source of wellness. A sincere smile is one way to do this, on the job and throughout the day.

7. Sometimes Time Flies and Sometimes It Creeps

Is there anything more subjective than time? I was leaving my workplace this afternoon when I heard one person say, "Wow, this day really flew by." And another person said, "Wow, I didn't think this day would ever end."

The perception of time varies not only among individuals but also with the tasks being performed. Sometimes I look at the clock and wonder where the day went; other times it seems like the clock must be broken, otherwise why would it say that only a few minutes have passed since the last time I checked.

Trying to come up with an explanation for this, I think it is related to satisfaction with the work. When I feel ownership over what I am doing, when I am immersed both intellectually and emotionally, I am more fulfilled and time never stalls. When my work connects to a larger vision and everyone is cooperative and amiable, time passes well.

Physicists can give us an explanation of time in a physical sense, even write equations proving it. But the experience is defined by us. It goes quickly when we are having fun, are being creative, are enthused, or are engaged. And it goes slowly when distractions or negativity take us off-course, we feel lost or confused or we experience disunity.

German philosopher Immanuel Kant noted the subjectivity of time when he wrote:

> *Time is not something objective. It is neither substance nor accident nor relation, but a subjective condition, necessary owing to the nature of the human mind.*[13]

Whether we perceive time as fast or slow, it doesn't wait for us. If there is a due date for an assignment or project, it will arrive. As when a child throws a ball and shouts "Ready or not, here it comes," much of what we are working on has urgency to it. This is true at the workplace, and it is true about the world-at-large.

Given the state of our environment and the already-present impact of climate change, time doesn't wait. Immediate action is needed, and delays are devastating as well as costly.

Wherever people are starving, time doesn't wait. One more day without sufficient food may be the day that their health takes a turn that cannot be reversed.

Wherever there is war, every day brings death, destruction, and the intensification of emotions. There are children who have never known peace or brotherhood with other people, and for them time doesn't wait.

Shoghi Effendi, in addressing the Bahá'ís about their role in bringing unity, justice, peace, and community to the world, wrote:

> *The sands are indeed running out. . . The distractions, temptations, and pitfalls that might interfere with its consummation are many and varied.*[14]

Each day when we wake, we begin with opportunities. And then, when we prepare for sleep and reflect on how the day went, we are fortunate when we can say, "Time passed well, and I am happy with how I lived today." We know that this life is finite and every day has 24 hours. What we put into those hours, what we take from them, is where we exercise our free will. Whatever time feels like, we have the choice to use it well or not.

8. Needed: Better (Not Just More) Communications

Enthused about an idea for a project, I mentioned it to an acquaintance at an out-of-town event. She liked the idea and had some suggestions for follow-up. I did my homework and got back to her by email a couple of weeks later. In her reply she asked if we could continue the discussion by phone instead. So over the next three days we played phone tag, missing each other time and again. Even when we agreed on a specific time for a call, something or other got in the way.

Finally, we had our conversation today, and I asked her why she had insisted on telephone rather than email. She said that she prefers talking with people, that too many nuances and cues are missing in email. Okay, I do understand her point, though one could also say that a telephone call is lacking compared to talking face-to-face. Yet other people might argue the opposite, claiming that the time delay inherent in email allows better consideration of ideas. We could also throw into the mix the possibility of texting or skype for real-time communications. Or even the ways it used to be done, i.e. via letters, memo, and meetings.

Whew — communication is complicated with so many choices! Do options and convenience indicate improvement in communication effectiveness? Does change mean progress?

In the mid-1800s Henry David Thoreau wrote:

> *All our inventions are but improved means to an unimproved end.*[15]

As witty and insightful as this is, and respected as Thoreau may be as a thinker and author, I do find it rather cynical. Nevertheless, this quotation is a reminder about the difference between development and progress. An invention may have technological significance, but that doesn't mean it helps us achieve our goals any better than its predecessors.

Moving to more recent times, we have Marshall McLuhan, whose words have become embedded in our culture:

The medium is the message.[16]

And with an almost contrary stance, we might also consider words from today's high-tech thinkers and leaders such as Mark Kvamme:

No new medium ever completely replaces another. Even cave paintings haven't gone away — we just call them graffiti.[17]

Ideas such as these converge around the basic question as to the very nature of communications. At its essence, it is an innate characteristic of being human. Whatever may be the truth about the medium, the message, and innovation — we need to communicate.

Bahá'u'lláh predicted an increased range of communications and its role in creating unity. As summarized by Shoghi Effendi:

The unity of the human race . . . implies the establishment of a world commonwealth in which all nations, races, creeds and classes are closely and permanently united . . . A mechanism of world inter-communication will be devised, embracing the whole planet, freed from national hindrances and restrictions, and functioning with marvellous swiftness and perfect regularity.[18]

Our communications may be spoken, written, broadcast, or otherwise expressed. In any case, we may check for coherence between words and deeds. Is there energy and commitment? When other people are involved, do we listen and persist until we have reconciled differences? Is there congruence, i.e. are the outer form and inner essence in harmony? Is there power in the communications — power derived from sincere concern for others?

In these days of so many ways to communicate, quantity is easily confused with quality. In the meantime, I ask myself these sorts of questions and check to see if I'm on track for communications that can make a difference.

9. Work Without a Job

Currently between jobs, I am fortunate that, for awhile anyway, I am not worried about being without an income. This is a welcome and rare opportunity to reconsider how I spend my time and where I put my energy. Subject to practical limitations, there are many possibilities.

People are jobless for lots of reasons, sometimes intentionally. The reason may be retirement, a leave of absence for travel, further education or professional development, or a hiatus between contracts. At other times though, it isn't so welcome, with unemployment being stressful and bringing hardship.

Whatever the reason and however long it may last, it does offer a chance to reflect on various matters. For me now, a phrase from the Báb keeps going through my mind:

> . . . *in my work or in my occupation* . . .[19]

This has me considering the difference between occupation (or job) and work. If job is what I do for money, then work is what I do for myself and others. If job is about making a living, then work is about living. If a job has a beginning and an end, then work is ongoing.

The Bahá'í Faith teaches that action performed in the spirit of service is a form of worship, and being paid money does not detract from the genuineness of the attitude in which it is done. I realize that even while on the job, there was work to do, even if sometimes it was hard to connect it all while meeting daily demands.

Admittedly, at times the distinction between these two words seems to blur, with both related to fulfilling the purpose of life. Our true work is about self-improvement and contributing to social progress. Whatever may be my own potential to contribute to the greater good — that is my work.

Phrases from 'Abdu'l-Bahá about the purpose of life include ideas such as:

> *brighten the whole world of humanity . . . live in unity, concord and agreement . . . love one another . . . acquire virtues*[20]

Humans are innately social and outward looking. This means we can demonstrate our commitment to unity and love through being friendly without prejudice, working for justice, and aligning ourselves with noble ideals. Being engaged in arts and sciences is another way to do this — by expressing ourselves creatively or finding a better way to do something. These sorts of actions contribute to brightening humanity, even as we improve our own characters and acquire virtues.

Humans are like a lamp whose purpose is not fulfilled until it shines its light. Similarly, our purpose — our work — is to find the source of that light and then illumine the way for others. Deep within ourselves we know that our lives are meant to be more than just pleasure seeking. We might say that being grateful for the pleasures of life is a spiritual quality and then moving beyond pleasure is a sign of spiritual maturity. Being actively involved in life outside of our own self-interest, studies confirm, is a key factor in both longevity and maintaining a positive self-concept.

At least for awhile, I have time to reconsider who I am, what I want to do, and what impact my actions may have. This is a precious time, and I am grateful to have the chance to reflect on both my job and my work.

10. A Time for Change

A friend of my family has just retired from her job, having worked at the same place for over 35 years. Though I suppose this is not an unusual thing to do, most of the people I know have changed jobs or even their careers at least once. Some make the changes willingly, while others do so in response to external events. Some have employers, others are self-employed. The variations are countless. Whatever may be the career path any of us follow, every choice we make leaves behind all the choices we didn't make.

A person like my friend who commits to one employer offers not only her daily work but also strength through consistency, continuity, and institutional history. And while that is not the path I followed, I do think that its value is frequently overlooked in our fast-paced, disposable, youth-oriented culture. A similar situation occurs when people live in one place for many years, perhaps even for a lifetime. They help anchor the entire community in its own roots, even if that is a mixed metaphor.

I asked my friend her reflections on 35 years at the same place. She was quick to say that much had changed over the years — both within the employer and within herself. I suppose it is inevitable that a workplace over such a long period would have undergone changes, possibly in the very nature of the work itself. Beyond the daily work and range of responsibilities, and even beyond integration of technology, areas such as ownership, management style, the provision of benefits, and social dynamics may have changed.

These changes reflect a shift in consciousness and social progress. Even a brief look at each shows us why. Technology at its best can help shorten the workday. Ownership and management style can offer employees a chance to participate in profits. Benefits can improve health and lifestyle. Social dynamics might be inclusive of women and minorities in a meaningful way. These changes have the potential to align the workplace with higher principles, though fulfillment of that potential may yet be off in the future.

Change is a characteristic of life, not just our jobs. Seasons change; life begins then grows then dies; the planet itself shifts then settles just to shift again. Bob Dylan elegantly summarized this fact through this well-known line:

> *The Times They Are a-Changin'*[21]

He may have been commenting on social action and change for the young adults of his own generation, but the words continue to resonate. They persist in pop culture because of the truth they tell.

Countless others have commented on change as being a constant in our lives. I especially like these words from Winston Churchill, because they are a reminder that change in and of itself is neither good nor bad:

> *There is nothing wrong with change, if it is in the right direction.*[22]

Recognizing the difference between conditions that are inward and those that are outward, the Bahá'í Writings distinguish between spiritual truths and social teachings. Spiritual truths are timeless and have been reconfirmed by each of the Divine Messengers. Through these same Messengers, social teachings — relevant to the times — are given to humanity so that we can advance our thinking, our conduct, and our practical affairs.

Bahá'u'lláh addressed this point by writing:

> *The wisdom of this is that the times never remain the same, for change is a necessary quality and an essential attribute of this world, and of time and place.*[23]

A life decision such as retiring from a job brings change. In fact, everyone experiences change as we journey through this life, whether we consciously seek it or not. Some people welcome change, some resist it, and some even resent it. But none of us can avoid it.

II. Volunteering — Paid with More than Money

What contributes to quality as well as quantity of life? To our happiness and our longevity? That is a question I have been actively researching. Some obvious items appear high on most lists, for example good health practices and strong social support systems. But another item that is cropping up in reports from recent studies is volunteering.

People can and do volunteer at all stages of life and of varying duration. Even within elder years, it is often part of retirement plans.

Pop culture and TV commercials give the impression that retirement is primarily about hobbies, travel, cultural interests, and personal indulgences. I agree that it should offer a chance for those sorts of pleasure. But there is more to consider, notably to volunteer; to give time without financial incentive or reward is a wonderful, life-affirming experience.

Unless someone is born wealthy (and often even in that case), for much of our lives having a job for income is normal, desirable, and necessary. Some people love their jobs, many don't. Yet most of us want and need jobs and recognize this as having a role in meeting our responsibilities as adults.

Though many of us volunteer our time and skills during our working years, not everyone is able to do so, or at least not often. There can be genuine and practical barriers. Without judging other people's circumstances or decisions, I am now exploring the yearning to volunteer and why that is so satisfying.

The word "volunteer" offers a clue, as it comes from the Latin word for "of one's free will." Even if we are busy and faced with distractions as well as diversions, we willingly donate our time. Something seems to motivate us, to offer an intrinsic reward or incentive.

Clearly money is not the only way of being paid. Rather, we frequently feel that we receive more than we give when we donate time for a worthy cause or otherwise sacrifice for others. We cannot quantify it, but we feel gratified by helping someone live better, giving comfort to someone in need, rescuing an animal, planting trees, cleaning up a road or park, stuffing envelopes — whatever may be the volunteer activity. It feels good because it is good.

Ask people what they would do if they were suddenly extremely wealthy, and "I'd give some of it away" is often part of the answer. We enjoy donating money in support of a cause in which we believe. Just as good or even better, we can donate our time, energy, and know-how.

'Abdu'l-Bahá talked about generosity being an element of all faiths and then connected it to our progress:

> All religions teach that we must do good, that we must be generous, sincere, truthful, law-abiding, and faithful; all this is reasonable, and logically the only way in which humanity can progress.[24]

Economists are developing ways to evaluate the impact of volunteerism through the lens of social capital. This attempts to validate, through objective metrics, the contributions people make to their communities and society through nonfinancial, nonmaterial means. Anyone who has volunteered their time and seen what these acts can do already knows what economists are learning to measure.

'Abdu'l-Bahá connected service to humanity as one of the means to nearness to God:

> . . . nearness to God is possible through devotion to Him, through entrance into the Kingdom and service to humanity; it is attained by unity with mankind and through loving-kindness to all; it is dependent upon investigation of truth, acquisition of praiseworthy virtues,

service in the cause of universal peace and personal sanctification.[25]

Somehow we know, deep within ourselves, that to volunteer is to help humanity. It brings joy, it brings satisfaction. The rewards are tremendous, and they are tax-free.

Chapter 4
Health and Recreation

I. Strength and Balance from My Core

While treating me for a back and hip injury, my physiotherapist recommended I take some Pilates classes. Through his clinic, I enrolled in a series specially conducted for people with back issues similar to mine.

I had already been introduced to Pilates through fitness instructors incorporating a few movements into our routines. But this is my first time to experience it so fully, with the result that I finally understand the difference between "abs" and "core" in a literal, physical sense.

As the word itself suggests, a person's core is deep inside. Related to both balance and strength, it is often overlooked in favor of other, more visually obvious muscle groups. I found myself thinking about the word "core" as symbolic of my own spiritual self. And soon I discovered many parallels.

My core self is what holds everything else in place. Though invisible to the eye, a weakness within it is readily detected when life feels out of balance and confusing. When I know who I am and what I am doing; when I am both confident and resolute: then my core is intact.

A strong physical core protects other muscles from injury, and a strong core self protects me from harmful thoughts and actions. It does this by being the locus of my most important beliefs. This in turn is the source of my integrity to the extent that my actions reflect my beliefs.

Strengthening my physical core requires time and commitment to a series of exercises. Among the mechanisms for doing this for my core self are thoughtful reflection, study, open-mindedness, consultation with others, and perceptiveness.

To be physically balanced means to coordinate body parts. Within my core self, it means being coordinated with other personal qualities. John Kolstoe offers this list from a Bahá'í perspective:

The highest kind of strength, confidence and reliance in one's relationship to God is required to maintain the balance.[1]

My relationship to God, as mentioned in that quote, is the key to this entire discussion. The motivation for strengthening my core self, the practices for doing it, the focus of the results — all are linked to my own spiritual self. The connection to my Creator is ultimately what is inside of me and is what comprises the real me.

And to explore yet one more dimension, Anne Morrow Lindbergh offers this thought about the relationship of my own core to other people:

Only when one is connected to one's own core is one connected to others.[2]

Returning to the Pilates exercises themselves, sometimes they are not especially exciting. So much of the time I'd rather do something more active. And yet I know that discipline and patience will bring results. This may require setting aside other activities that are otherwise tempting or distracting, but I am motivated by confidence in the outcome.

In contrast, the exercises required for my core self are never boring and never finished for the week. So this is where the comparison between physical core and core self falls apart. I strengthen my core self through daily living: being happy in all circumstances; being grateful for my life and its blessing; feeling compassion; expressing love through service; and taking time for study, prayer, and meditation.

There is yet another possibility. I can invite a friend to join me in study or prayer. Similar to physical exercises where people counterbalance each other's weight, the result will be that both of us will become more strong and balanced — all the way to the core.

2. Energy from Happiness

When I need an energy boost, I have lots to choose from. Coffee, juice, fresh fruit, energy bars — sometimes even just a glass of water gives me what I need. During a phone conversation with a friend this morning, another idea was mentioned: drawing energy from happiness.

We didn't deny the obvious need for food, drink, and rest to revive our weary bodies. Rather, we were exploring how happiness might be the source of energy for the oomph needed to greet each day with fresh enthusiasm. We agreed that happiness can pump spiritual energy directly into us.

There is no simple explanation to what makes a person happy. Some folks are happy when they are working, others when they are relaxing. Some are enriched through music and the arts, others through family gatherings. Some enjoy museums and galleries, others thrive best in nature. Some like to be surrounded by other people, others seek solitude. The variations are endless.

However and wherever each of us seeks our own happiness, we are drawn to its source, much like a magnetic field. 'Abdu'l-Bahá recognized this tendency in saying:

> *When a man has found the joy of life in one place, he returns to that same spot to find more joy . . . This shows the internal force and natural instinct which God has given to man, and the power of vital energy which is born in him.*[3]

Thinking about what makes people happy, I put the word "love" at the top of the list. Love is the universal source of happiness in both the physical and the spiritual realms. As 'Abdu'l-Bahá said:

Thoughts of love are constructive of brotherhood, peace, friendship, and happiness.[4]

Despite the word itself having been romanticized to the point of sounding trite or even corny, love warms our hearts and guides our highest deeds. Beyond love for family and friends, it extends to our planet itself and its creatures. As such it is both animating and motivating.

In addition to experiencing love, we are happy when we have daily purpose. We are energized through knowing that we have something significant to do each day. Not all of us are blessed with jobs that we like, but recognizing within that job the opportunity to learn and grow, to strive for excellence, to earn the material means to support ourselves — these thoughts can infuse us with renewed vigor. Beyond our jobs there are so many other ways we spend our days, and if our actions are meaningful then we are energized by them.

Helping others brings happiness. From volunteering an afternoon for a local cleanup project to offering a seat to someone on a bus or train, assisting others makes us happy. As a bonus, the more unexpected or spontaneous the better, since it comes as such a welcome surprise.

We know about the connection between our minds and our bodies. When one of them feels droopy then so does the other. To a great extent though, we can willfully overcome this — since the mind rules the body. Just to offer one example, consider someone who is physically sick yet maintains a positive attitude and their sense of humor. This returns us to the idea of fueling ourselves through spiritual happiness as a source of energy.

I can't buy happiness in a wrapped package at the grocery or find it in a vitamin pill at the pharmacy. But if I want to, I can create it by myself. And a daily dose is all that is required to energize me.

3. Advice Along the Trail

Walking along a trail over the weekend, I noticed a series of benches with commemorative plaques. I thought about how they all have a story, a reason why someone was remembered in this way. And then one in particular caught my attention. It read, "Remember, we are all artists."

Me? An artist? I can't draw. My 2nd grade teacher told me I wasn't any good, and I believed her. As I continued along the trail, I remembered a string of teachers, coaches, and other adults over my school years who had given me a similarly negative message and how limiting they were.

Yet on another, higher level, I do know that the phrase on the bench is true. We are all artists if we define "artist" as a person with the potential for expression through a creative medium.

Pablo Picasso obviously realized the innate creativity within everyone — and the unfortunate fact that this is often inhibited or even squashed by others. He wrote:

> *Every child is an artist. The problem is how to remain an artist once we grow up.*[5]

A problem indeed! I think a big part of the problem is that teachers such as the one I had in 2nd grade, or the coaches who didn't find me particularly strong or coordinated, underestimate the effect they can have on children. Just because my artwork isn't likely to end up in a gallery doesn't mean I'm not an artist; and just because I'm not athletically gifted doesn't mean I can't find a way to participate in and enjoy sports.

The Writings frequently mention encouraging children to pursue their potential in all endeavors, including the arts. During many Bahá'í community gatherings and events, the arts play a key role — with the infusion of music, visual, and performance arts.

In a paper on community development, the Bahá'í International Community built a link between spiritual education, which includes creativity, and self-sufficiency. This excerpt says it well:

> *Spiritual education, which helps to develop qualities such as enthusiasm, dedication, creativity and service, along with the practical skills, leads to self-sufficiency.*[6]

Considering the relationship between creativity and community development, we find that self-sufficiency leads to higher self-esteem, which in turn can lead to having the confidence to share ideas with friends, to speak at meetings, to participate in public discourse, to join in group projects, and to otherwise engage in collective and community life. In other words, the impulse to create can be expressed in many and diverse venues.

Underlying this entire discussion is recognition of other people's worthiness and dignity. This recognition unleashes creativity and the realization of potential. It also results in a more supportive environment, since in an overly competitive society only the most talented are praised. In its place we can have cooperation and an exchange of ideas through the arts.

Accepting the idea that "we are all artists" invites us to broaden our definition of the word "artists" and to acknowledge that we are all capable, creative, and expressive. It says that we care about what others create without feeling compelled to compare or judge. It transforms us into explorers and innovators, and it allows us to become masters of our own crafts.

Perhaps most importantly, it would help us turn off the inner doubts that were planted by others. If we believe the message on the bench — "we are all artists" — then we are.

4. Beyond Training: Doing

I love being physically active, and I'm fortunate to be able to work out almost every day. And even though I'm not athletic in a competitive sense, I do occasionally register for an event for fun or fund-raising.

Overall though, my workouts are for fitness, in contrast to people who are training for a competition or a team sport. Considering the difference between our reasons for being there, I have been thinking lately about the distinction between preparing and performing, between training and doing.

Athletes train. Musicians practice. Artists sketch. Actors rehearse. Inventors test. Students study. Writers draft. But sooner or later, it's time to DO whatever all this preparation has been about.

Regardless of the time and effort put into training, *doing* is a different experience, frequently harder — it's supposed to be. For example, I can manage the routines and drills in a group cycling class. Yet, on a rough outdoor trail, I might walk my bike uphill and use my brakes downhill for fear of missing a curve. I can swim laps for a mile without stopping. Nevertheless, I'm pretty sure that in open water I couldn't complete a mile, at least not without a great deal of struggle. And even though I lift weights, I still need John's help in opening jars.

This is how life works, as we have experiences that prepare us for greater challenges in the future. How we do in those preparations is reflected in how we handle the challenges (tests) later. And since the tests will require us to go further than we did while training, we feel satisfied when we get a chance to perform our best, at whatever we have been practicing.

Martha Graham, renowned dancer and choreographer, elevated practicing to a spiritual realm by writing:

> *We learn by practice. Whether it means to learn to dance*
> *by practicing dancing or to learn to live by practicing*

living, the principles are the same. One becomes in some area an athlete of God.[7]

This quotation links to a larger question: What are we preparing for by living this life? Since we are spiritual beings, one of the purposes of this life is to prepare us for the next. A human embryo cannot envision what this world is like, but it grows physically in its journey toward birth. Similarly, I cannot know what the next world will be like, but I am moving toward it just the same.

Recognizing that this life is a journey to the next enriches my experiences with meaning and purpose. Life in this sense is training, or practice, for what comes next. Through the exercise of my free will I can improve and grow; I can advance my spiritual development.

We humans live both privately and publicly, and through our deeds we show who we are. As 'Abdu'l-Bahá said:

You are the reality and expression of your deeds and actions.[8]

As a writer, I believe that words can be inspiring and motivating. But the end results — attitude and actions — will reveal our integrity. It is easy to be cynical in these times. We are tested by political divisiveness, crime, economic hardship, and environmental degradation. On the other hand, if we were to view these tests as practice, if we were to consider them as training for both this world and the next, then we will see them in a different way.

On any given day I can go the gym, work hard, and enjoy being there — or not. In other words, I can choose how I want to train my body. Similarly, I can willfully expand my mind through study, informed conversation, and other kinds of intellectual training.

What ultimately endures though is how I develop my character. I may not be able to choose how I am tested, but I do have control over how I face my tests. Perhaps it sounds too simple to say it all happens through practice. Yet that is how it works.

5. A Balanced Diet for Eating and Living

My inbox often includes several newsletters featuring breaking news, stories, ideas, and special offers. Too busy to read them in detail, I tend to scan for items of personal interest such as health and fitness. Sometime this turns out to be a super-duper diet plan or fitness regime or both. And then a few issues later there is yet another idea that is supposedly better. But one piece of advice that seems to persist is to eat a balanced diet.

Simple as that sounds, there are at least two major problems with it. Firstly, we do not have general agreement about what "balanced" means. And secondly, there can be obstacles to following it. To mention just a few of these: confusion, misinformation, lack of resources, and social pressure. So it isn't as easy as it sounds, but still we try because we know that balance is a worthy goal.

Every day brings the chance to be balanced, and not just in our food and health habits. Ultimately this idea of balance serves as advice for living in a healthful, wholesome way.

We hear a lot these days about life-work balance, generally thought to be a modern concern, prompted by our hectic times. As I have recently learned though, it is not a new concern, with the idea itself originating in the mid-1800s through the discipline of anthropology. And then the phrase "work-life-balance" was coined in the late-1970s in the UK and the mid-1980s in the US.

When I learned that it isn't such a new idea after all, I realized that it coincided with industrialism, mechanization, and technological advancement. It seems that, as our material lives have advanced, so has the tension between work (on-the-job time) and life (the rest of the time). The irony is that money — as the material outcome of work — has not brought the free time that might help us become more balanced.

Sometimes I feel like I'm back in math class, trying to balance an equation!

Looking further into the "life" part of this equation, I see many aspects of life that need to be balanced. We need to take care of ourselves physically, intellectually, emotionally, and spiritually. We need time to be alone as well as with others. We need time to relax, have fun, and enjoy arts and culture. We do not want to be continuously driven to produce concrete results or meet other people's expectations.

Discussing these ideas not only from an individual perspective but also at a global level, 'Abdu'l-Bahá told us about the future:

> *Moderation, without which the truly balanced life is impossible, is a vital feature of the civilization now dawning upon humanity.*[9]

And in 1947, Shoghi Effendi wrote in a letter to an individual:

> *We believe in balance in all things; we believe in moderation in all things . . .*[10]

Both quotations support the idea that moderation is integral to balancing. As in the balanced diet approach to food, all components should be present in moderation to achieve the best outcome. This discussion is similar to exploring the balance between science and religion. Both have value, but if not balanced we can find ourselves trapped in either materialism or superstition.

Looking at the larger trends within our current society, there are many signs of our being out of balance. These include debt from excessive materialism, deteriorating health and morale, harmful prejudices, and extremes of poverty and wealth. A spiritually enlightened society would not tolerate these unjust conditions.

How do we overcome the ills of imbalance which have resulted from immoderation and injustice? It begins with the individual. The Universal House of Justice has explained the reciprocal relationship between individuals and society:

If an individual violates the spiritual laws for his own development he will cause injury not only to himself but to the society in which he lives. Similarly, the condition of society has a direct effect on the individuals who must live within it.[11]

This makes it clear that my own conduct, lifestyle, and social interactions will have a cumulative effect. As I strive for moderation and balance with other people and the planet, I will grow healthier, as will my community. And since a healthy community values the wellness of everyone, it will have a positive influence on yet other communities.

There is no better plan, no super-duper scheme that will be announced in next month's newsletter. We already know what to do. It may take time, but we can do it — if we stay balanced.

6. Over the Hills and Around the Curves of Life

On a bike ride with John last weekend, I had trouble with some of the hills and curves and was frankly relieved to find an easier, alternative route at one point of the trail. I turned my bike to follow it, and John waved as he took the more difficult option. Oh he's just showing off, I told myself, and he'll later wish he'd joined me on this one instead.

Well, I was wrong — as I saw a few minutes later when he soared down the other side of the hill, laughing in exhilaration at his achievement and the joy of overcoming the obstacles.

This reminded me of the rewards of meeting difficulties head-on. Which of us is more competent for yet another challenge? Which of us improved that day? Who is ready for further growth? Who went home feeling more fulfilled from the day's adventures?

Clichés such as "Nothing ventured, nothing gained" and "No pain, no gain" come to mind. If we lived without tests, if our lives were completely at ease, we would not experience personal growth and probably even be bored. And in any case, unlike difficult bike trails, *real* tests cannot be avoided; they are intrinsic to human existence.

Through tests we are strengthened, much like steel being tempered by fire or a muscle being trained for endurance. And through tests we learn who we are and have a chance to improve. This has potentially larger impact, as the Bahá'í International Community explained in a paper exploring several related concepts:

> . . . the growth of the individual must go hand in hand
> with the transformation of society. When individuals
> develop moral capacities and spiritual qualities, the

*skills and knowledge they acquire are likely to promote
the well-being of the community as a whole.*[12]

Drawing again on the metaphor about steel and muscles, we know that eventually the fire has done its job and the steel needs to cool; likewise, the muscle must rest and heal after exertion. Life is this way, too. Our difficulties finally pass, leaving us to absorb the lessons they gave us and to remember them when we need them another time.

On a personal level, I will improve and become better equipped to help others by engaging in the field of action and not being afraid of taking some risks. I may be only a tiny part of our community life, but we all have a role to play, and the better and stronger each of us is then the better for all.

In my early days as a Bahá'í (I was in my 30s) I was surprised to find some prayers wherein one asks for tests — like it's a good thing and something we should seek. I admit, I didn't understand what this was all about. Yet another section included prayers seeking assistance with tests, and that made more sense to me.

But as time passed and I not only experienced but also reflected on easy as well as difficult times, I gradually saw the wisdom. To pray for tests is to want to become stronger and be prepared to face life's inevitable challenges, much like John enjoying the hills and curves on a bike trail. I think next time I'll join him. I might fall, or I might make the curves. In either case, I'll be the better for it — and might have some fun, too.

7. Hobbies and Amateurs — Loving Deeds

"I made it, but it's just a hobby," the woman mumbled to me when I admired her necklace. She said it as if confessing guilt over something, implying that a hobby is somehow inferior to a profession or a job. Yet during the many years she has been making jewelry, she has created pieces that are as lovely as items sold in stores. She doesn't sell her creations; she wears them herself or gives them as gifts. That makes her a hobbyist and an amateur rather than a professional — at least that's what the words literally mean.

The problem is that the labels "hobby" and "amateur" can sound judgmental. We hear statements such as "He behaved like a real pro" and "He was amateurish." And through the nuances of our language we interpret the first as a good thing and the second as a bad thing — or at least not as good as the first.

The usual distinction is that professionals get paid and amateurs do not. We are paid for doing our jobs and spend many (sometimes too many) hours doing them. Hobbies are typically outside of work and unpaid, which seemingly demotes them in value.

Yet, considering that the root of the word "amateur" is "love," it seems to me that receiving some specific quantity of time or monetary payment is not always better than doing something out of love.

Gain in social status is a reward often seen within sports and its major and minor leagues. Relative to minor leagues, major league events have higher ticket prices and generate more advertising revenue. They create more excitement, and they offer fame to the athletes.

And then there is the entertainment world, which reveres reveres Hollywood, Bollywood, Broadway, London's West End, and other such high-profile venues over community theatre. And yet, beyond the star appeal of professional sports and award-winning performances we have smaller-scale, community-based events. These grassroots activities are more accessible, more universal. In the absence of material reward there are other satisfactions. The joy of performing is matched by the joy of observing.

I recognize and respect that people who perform, compete, and create as a profession have gotten there through talent and perseverance. Nevertheless, I find something admirable, even noble, about people who do this out of a loving impulse without regard to tangible reward. Similar to volunteerism, the motivation is intrinsic rather than extrinsic.

During my university years, I knew a man who sang opera as a hobby. Before I met him, he had sung professionally, but the rigors of the business itself reduced his joy. However, since he loved singing, he didn't stop. Instead, he rented private rehearsal space and sang for pleasure. Singing was part of who he was as a person.

Marzieh Gail wrote:

> *One can judge a man by what he loves . . . this type of man has always enriched his fellows, and when he dies, the flowers are a little fresher over him, and other men come, and sit by his grave, and remember what he was.*[13]

In the Bahá'í Faith, actions performed through love are a form of service and prayer. And while we would hope that through our jobs and other professional work we can feel and express love at that level, this is not always the case.

A woman who makes beautiful jewelry in her spare time, a person who coaches little league, and anyone with a hobby — all are amateurs, motivated by love. To me they are real pros, even if they can only find a few minutes a day in which to do it and no one pays them money for it.

8. Health, Disease, and Dis-Ease

This week I have learned about three people being diagnosed with cancer, bringing to 11 the number I personally know with this mysterious disease. And it is not the only disease I'm hearing about, as I know other people with other ailments, some serious and some less so. I consider them all within the idea of "dis-ease" in the sense of not being in a state of wellness.

According to family stories, I was maybe six years old when I learned that one of my uncles had the title "Doctor" because of his advanced degree in economics. "Does this mean the economy is sick?" I asked, probably not even knowing what "the economy" was.

My childhood naiveté did have a point to it though. Not only our physical bodies but also our minds and our social institutions can be healthy, sick, or somewhere in-between.

I don't have the expertise to explain cancer (or any disease), nor do I know why it seems to be so much more common than in the past. It clearly isn't restricted to any specific age group, gender, ethnic background, geographic region, or set of behaviors. Yes, there can be contributing factors, but there is so much more to it than that.

On a more abstract level, whether we are talking about a person's health, a community's well-being, or an ailing social institution, the principles through which a cure is sought may be the same. And lacking a cure, well — what can we learn about managing dis-ease?

The Bahá'í Writings advise seeking healing through both spiritual and material means. The spiritual means include actions such as prayer, meditation, and surrounding oneself with positive influences. Some specific examples of these include being in nature, music and other arts, and uplifting social connections.

Material means include seeking competent medical advice and using our own intellect to engage in the conversation about our care. Great emphasis is placed on healthy foods, clean water, physical activity, and abstinence from nonprescribed drugs and intoxicants.

Combining the spiritual and the material means and then applying them to a social level, there are several strategies to adopt. The first is learning from experts. What does current research offer? What would be the advice of a panel of experts, seeking truth without ego? With no shortage of people with knowledge and insights, we need them to come together in a spirit of interdisciplinary, nonpartisan cooperation.

Another strategy is citizen engagement in evaluating policy and coordinating action. As important as input from experts might be, citizens and other stakeholders deserve a venue for input, with confidence that their opinions will be considered. The challenge can be balancing individual interests with the greater good, but at the very least everyone should have a voice.

Engaging in a wide range of means of expression and including diverse peoples will bring in perspectives that might otherwise be missed. Seeing things from different viewpoints augments the input from experts, whose specific training would then be complemented by others.

Ultimately, the most important ways to address social ills is to think in terms of the greater good and to believe in the future. Optimism, rather than pessimism or cynicism, is needed. Otherwise the whole endeavor is doomed from the start.

'Abdu'l-Bahá compared mankind as a collective entity to a sick or ailing human body, a body in need of healing. And he said that the teachings of Bahá'u'lláh are the remedy.

> . . . today these heavenly Teachings are the remedy for a
> sick and suffering world, and a healing balm for the sores
> on the body of mankind. They are the spirit of life . . . the
> dynamic power to motivate the inner self of man.[14]

Like physical and mental diseases, social ills are complex. Being mindful of what contributes to physical health and managing disease can guide us in our work toward building a healthier future for all people and for our planet. And given the relationship between the two, a healthier planet will contribute to greater physical and mental health among its people. That would lesson our collective dis-ease in its many forms.

9. Life Is a HIIT

No, that's not a typo in the title. An acronym for "high intensity interval training," HIIT is a training technique for running and other sports that has been incorporated into group fitness classes. The idea is simple enough: alternating periods of high exertion with shorter periods of rest. One of my favorite versions calls for doing a specific exercise at peak intensity for 20 seconds and then 10 seconds of rest, this pattern to be repeated eight times. And then another round with a different exercise, and so on. There are conceivably dozens of variations that work, but the idea is always the same.

Even though I know it is good for me, sometimes I have to convince myself to go one more round. I remind myself that the greatest improvement comes from what I do after I wish I could stop. And in those situations I find that it is mental as much as physical exercise.

Life itself happens in a similar way, though rarely in burst just a few seconds long or in that 2:1 ratio. Still, the comparison holds if we consider that times of difficulties are sandwiched by times of rest and recovery. Key elements are accepting the inevitability of tests, anticipating satisfaction when finished, and believing in improvement through the process.

As Shoghi Effendi wrote:

> *Life is a process of trials and testings, and these are —*
> *contrary to what we are prone to thinking — good for*
> *us, and give us stamina, and teach us to rely on God.*
> *Knowing He will help us, we can help ourselves more.*[15]

While doing my HIIT workout I sometimes think of the children's story *The Little Engine That Could*, changing the line "I think I can, I think I can" to "I *know* I can, I *know* I can." Positive self-talk helps build confidence and distracts from discomfort. My mind tells my body to keep going, knowing that the more I do the better I will get. This is a maturing process, helping me to learn to persevere in other situations as well. If I can go breathless for yet another 20 seconds, then I will be stronger in meeting the challenges of my daily life.

Exercise is self-directed, and there are ways to cheat. But who gains if I cheat? No one will. Who loses if I do? I will. Being honest with myself is yet another way this activity influences my character. The phrase "honest sweat" fits here.

Life's tests present varying levels of intensity. Sometimes the test is relatively simple and short term, such as an annoying companion, an unpleasant event, or an inconvenient task. Other times though a test can feel crushing and never-ending. In these situations, we must trust that it will end, that a way will be found — even though presently we feel distraught, discouraged, and overwhelmed.

I enjoy exercising with others, as their presence keeps me motivated. Likewise, some of life's problems can be shared. We can confide in a friend, consult with others for clarity and inspiration, or turn to loved ones for comfort.

Ultimately though, the actual work is done at an individual level. No one can live my life for me, just as no one can exercise for me. And because of this, the rewards — satisfaction, relief, and growth — are mine to enjoy, too.

10. Being Healthy — Outside and In

Sitting in the waiting room of the doctor's office, I looked through the magazines on her table. Many were of general interest: gardening, fashion, sports. As I flipped through the pages of the magazines about health, I noticed two distinct categories: articles that were about physical health and those that were about mental health.

This got me wondering about health both outside and in. What determines each? What is the difference between them? How does one impact the other? What can I do to improve both?

Some of the articles explained that physical health is maintained or even improved through food, water, exercise, and rest. Each should be good quality and in the proper quantity, and each should be balanced with the other. That seems simple enough, though of course there is more to it.

Other articles discussed mental health. They reported that it is maintained or even improved through a positive attitude, a sense of purpose, love, clear thinking, and positive social connections. But as with physical health just mentioned, there is more to it.

For one thing, physical and mental, outer and inner, are not entirely separate within us; each influences the other. For example, we know that laughter is good for digestion, tears help to remove toxins, smiles and hugs make us feel warm inside, a fun evening helps us sleep, and worry can keep us up at night.

This Yiddish proverb humorously reminds us of the desirability of being healthy both ways:

What good is a good head if the legs won't carry it?[16]

A few years ago, I attended a BIBO workshop. What does that mean? "BIBO" is an acronym for "breathe in, breathe out." The obvious need to do that literally aside, that same pattern in daily living is subtler. It calls for balance and time to do what we enjoy. A familiar experience is being immersed in something we love, perhaps a hobby or the arts, and finding our body relaxed and our mood elevated. If the activity is challenging physically, we can try to explain it as a "runner's high" or endorphins. But the same thing can happen even in sedentary situations.

The explanation is that we're not just physical or mental beings but rather a blend of these interdependent elements. And there is a third component: we are also spiritual beings. The true nature of our spirit (or soul) is unknowable, as it transcends this earthly life. Yet we do know at least some of the ways to keep our spirits healthy. We can do so through prayer, meditation, forgiveness, and selfless love for others.

In social or collective activities, we can become our best, healthiest selves. In various arenas of life, when we cooperate with others at our highest level, then it is almost as if our coming together in companionship creates a new entity. The Universal House of Justice, drawing on words of 'Abdu'l-Bahá, wrote:

> . . . love each other, constantly encourage each other, work together, be as one soul in one body, and in so doing become a true, organic, healthy body animated and illumined by the spirit. In such a body all will receive spiritual health and vitality from the organism itself . . .[17]

No one is blessed with perfect physical health, and we all have times that challenge us mentally. Bringing the two into balance is a step toward congruence. We are healthy when our thoughts, words, and actions carry the same message. Beyond just consistency, there is integrity within this. We are who we are, and we express it through our daily living. This is a sign of being healthy — outside and inside.

II. During Times of Severe Tests

A friend with several family members undergoing serious health issues and other long-term difficulties has asked me, "How do I sustain my love of God during severe tests?"

Even though the troubles will eventually pass, albeit with unknown outcomes, while in the middle of such times we may have difficulty seeing beyond it all. Winston Churchill offered a few words of practical advice:

If you're going through hell, keep going.[18]

In the meantime, my own advice is to maintain faith while taking action.

When family members are afflicted with ill health: The Bahá'í Writings advise us to seek the best medical advice. Throughout the process we can have an active role in evaluating the advice. When all factors have been considered and a course of action agreed upon, it must be carefully followed. We can also recognize the role that love has in healing, surrounding the afflicted person with love. The combination of consistent care and spiritual healing is powerful. Regardless of the eventual outcome, we can be reassured by what we have done and trust in Divine assistance. This is an act of faith, coupled with real-world action.

When friends leave this life: Confronting the death of a friend requires us to suffer from the loss even as it reminds us of our own mortality. If we recognize not only that this life is fleetingly short but also that we have eternal souls, then our perspective might change. We continue to miss our friends even as we become at peace with their own path. Being reminded of our own mortality can be an impetus to live with more clear intention — improving our character and contributing to a better future for all. These are acts of faith, too.

When financial troubles mount: This does not mean that we are ignorant or lazy; rather, it might be indicative of larger social ills. Beyond the present problems will be an opportunity to realign our practical affairs and to establish a lifestyle that coordinates with material means. We may need to depend on others for assistance. Through this sometimes-humbling act, we will not only survive but also grow spiritually. Faith helps us to see the gift in the present and to see beyond our current problems. It can also help us orient ourselves within the larger scheme of things, to enlarge our vision.

When we are exhausted by daily demands: As 'Abdu'l-Bahá is reported to have said:

> *If thy daily living become difficult . . . Be patient in the time of affliction and trial, endure every difficulty . . . Verily this is the life of satisfaction, the spiritual existence, heavenly repose, divine benediction and the celestial table! Soon thy Lord will extenuate thy straitened circumstances even in this world.* [19]

We have this reassurance from The Universal House of Justice, paraphrasing statements from both Bahá'u'lláh and 'Abdu'l-Bahá:

> *God will not burden any soul beyond its capacity.*[20]

This is a reminder that somewhere, somehow — within each of us — is the capacity to face and even overcome whatever occurs. And we can keep in mind that everything is transitory, even life itself. With faith we know that what we are currently experiencing goes beyond simple labeling or judging.

Another aspect to this is that we learn and grow through sharing our troubles. Spiritual maturity is linked to recognizing that sometimes things happen not just for our own good but for the good of others. I see this as an element of friendship, i.e. sharing both good and bad, even as we learn and grow together. It's not that anyone would ever wish hardship on a friend, but being a companion to another person through their troubles is enlightening.

As a final thought, perhaps the most important aspect of faith is recognizing that what happens to us in this physical realm is related to — yet apart from — what happens to us in the spiritual realm. The human soul, mysterious and unknowable because of our limitations as humans, is always intact. Closing with another quotation from 'Abdu'l-Bahá:

> *Whatever his body has to suffer, his spirit is free and well!*[21]

Chapter 5
Arts and Culture

1. Making a Bucket List

Sometimes a movie introduces an idea or a phrase into everyday language. "Go ahead, make my day" and "May the Force be with you" are two classic examples. "Bucket list" is yet another, though it did not originate with the film by that title.[1] As is commonly known, it refers to a wish list of what we want to do before we leave this planet.

Ask someone what's on their bucket list, and they often mention exotic travel destinations, learning new things, collecting rare and beautiful items, daring adventures, and mending personal relationships. I have had my own list for years, though as I get older I find that my goals change. And, well, sometimes just daily living feels like enough. But I recently had a glimpse into another perspective on this, through the experience of one of my friends.

Attending a personal goals workshop, my friend was instructed to make a list of 100 things she wanted to achieve or experience in life. She readily thought of the first dozen, and with further effort she had a list of several more dozen. Though that was far from the 100 assigned, she was content — until a colleague challenged her to keep going, to go deeper. Much to her surprise, some of the last ones she thought of turned out to be the most important to her. They had to be dug out, as if they were gems being mined from deep in the earth.

Her story motivated me to update and expand my own list. And like her, I found some items that had previously been suppressed. As I thought about what they had in common, I concluded that they had been blocked by doubt or a lack of clarity.

If I have doubt or fear about something, then I might find even greater pleasure and satisfaction in doing it. Perhaps that sounds like an oversimplification, but by confronting my fears I can accomplish more than I may realize — so long as it's realistic. (I'm not likely to overcome my fears of wild animals and learn to be a lion tamer!) I can overcome doubt about meeting a physical challenge. I can achieve the intellectual challenge of learning a new language. I can buy the materials and pay for lessons for a new hobby. Goals that require time and commitment — if I have passion for them, if even thinking about them is exciting to me — are worthy of being moved toward the top of my bucket list.

Lack of clarity is another obstacle. A vague goal such as "get healthy" is too intangible. Likewise, "be more patient" has no substance and isn't measurable. What do they mean anyway? How would I know if I reach them?

If I know what the goal will look like and feel like, then I can take steps to make it happen. Bahá'u'lláh reminded us to be clear about what we are trying to do:

> At the outset of every endeavour, it is incumbent to look to the end of it.[2]

Not all goals are personal. Some involve my family or friends. Do they know that I have a goal that includes them? Do they agree with it? Are they working toward it, too? Unity in action is called for in these instances.

So long as we are alive, we aren't ever done. Whether my bucket list has 100 items on it or 10, life is an ongoing process. One goal achieved may lead to another. Another goal, even if not achieved, can be the stimulus for re-examining my priorities and my ever-changing life. This keeps the bucket list current and motivating.

Going back to my original list, the goals that I thought of first should not be overlooked just because they were so easy to think of. Many of them are just for fun — so why not do them? Come to think of it, I'm going to add to the top of my bucket list: Do something special every week, just for fun.

2. Every Day Is a Fresh Start

Gymnastics, both beautiful and thrilling to watch, is an event for the young — and sometimes the very young. This evening on TV, I saw a competition among gymnasts who were 7 and 8 years old. Midway through the program some of the children were interviewed. I was startled to hear one of the girls (I'll call her Laura) say, "I don't think I should have to compete against Cathy (also a made-up name). I already beat her yesterday."

I reminded myself that she's young, not yet schooled in how life works. She will mature, learn about life, and even be humbled by it. And one of the big lessons to learn is that one day's success is not the end of the story.

As stated by British-Austrian philosopher Ludwig Wittgenstein:

> *Resting on your laurels is as dangerous as resting when you are walking in the snow. You doze off and die in your sleep.*[3]

Laura hasn't yet learned that every day is a fresh start. When we get up in the morning we continue the path that ended the evening before, though we are not limited by it. We are not "done" just because we happened to win one day; nor are we doomed to failure just because that's what occurred the day before.

As we grow and mature, we learn that every day requires doing "it" again, whatever "it" is. We are not excused from showing up. Ironically, if we were to try this, our previous accomplishment might be interpreted as a fluke and our excellence might be labeled as sheer luck.

Elements of both progress and growth are also components of this situation. Through persistence, we might improve our results. Some of the ways we do this is through practicing, being coached or instructed, studying our competition, being motivated by our own potential, or changing strategies. We can also revise our goal to something more feasible yet still inspiring and challenging.

Laura doesn't yet grasp that on the other side of this story is another little girl who is eager to improve and give her own best performance another time. Feeling empathy for others, including our opponents, is a loving and generous attitude. Related to compassion and universal love, empathy means identifying with and understanding the reality of others. Through seeing the nobility of the other person, coupled with respect for the event itself, we become genuinely interested in our competitors and wish them well, win or lose.

Putting earthly events into time perspective, 'Abdu'l-Bahá wrote:

> ... in the sight of God the past, the present and the future are all one and the same ... relative to man, the past is gone and forgotten, the present is fleeting, and the future is within the realm of hope.[4]

And then continuing with this idea of each day being a fresh start and each event being a prelude to others, we might consider another passage from 'Abdu'l-Bahá. It tells us how this works, not just in sports and the arts:

> Mathematicians, astronomers, chemical scientists continually disprove and reject the conclusions of the ancients ... everything continually changing because human reason is progressing along new roads of investigation and arriving at new conclusions every day. In the future much that is announced and accepted as true now will be rejected and disproved. And so it will continue ad infinitum.[5]

Whatever our age, every day can take us forward — closer to our potential and nearer to our goals — whether we are concerned with sports, arts, business, innovation, or any other human endeavor. Through perseverance, optimism, recognition of the contributions of others, and the willingness to work with them, we can redefine what it means to win and discover the benefit of each day's fresh start.

3. Superheroes Among Us

Some of the most fun movies in recent years have been about superheroes. Many of the films showcase characters from earlier comics, while others introduce new ones. In either case, part of the appeal is that the films use new techniques in filmmaking, and the stories are situated in our present world.

In my own childhood, Superman was the dominant superhero in comics, television, and movies. And Supergirl was considered cool, too. Among the superheroes to have emerged over the years, some are from other planets (Superman); others are humans with acquired powers (Spiderman); still others are mutants (Wolverine); and so on. Whatever explanation is given for their powers, what they have in common is a desire to help rescue us regular folks from menacing, threatening situations.

Since pop culture mirrors its times, I've been thinking about what threatens us now. Almost every day we read or hear about crime, terrorism, wars, economic hardship, breakdown of family and social structures, divisive politics, and extreme weather. Frequently, similar to comics and films, it's a good guy vs. bad guy situation. More often though, the so-called "bad guy "is a nebulous group of people labeled "them." Or it may be a trend or prediction labeled "it."

In the presence of a specific event, such as a hurricane or an attack, real-life heroes emerge. Lacking Superman's powers, they nevertheless rise to the occasion and perform on an almost superhuman level. We may never learn their names or see their faces, but they work countless hours to protect us, clear debris, rescue people, restore power, remove dangerous chemicals, extinguish fires, and uplift others.

A list of heroes might include journalists who face great danger, even death, while covering stories about horrific wars. They ask difficult questions, and they challenge prevailing thought in pursuit of truth.

Also on the list might be some of today's scientists, researchers, and inventors — those who dare to think creatively and who risk their reputations and careers to pursue a grand idea.

And yes, there are other heroes. But on a more personal level, absent catastrophes or grandiose challenges, who can be a hero, even if not a superhero?

Helen Keller said:

> *The world is moved along, not only by the mighty shoves*
> *of its heroes, but also by the aggregate of tiny pushes of*
> *each honest worker.*[6]

These words remind us that our daily efforts can contribute to the world's betterment. Beyond movie images of heroism, beyond the win/lose proposition setup by video games, beyond comics that glorify battle — somewhere beyond that is space for everyday deeds. Circumstances may not be extraordinary, no one may see us, but our commitment and selflessness can and will make a difference.

The Bahá'í International Community in its 1992 *Earth Charter* document wrote:

> *The changes required to reorient the world toward a*
> *sustainable future imply degrees of sacrifice, social*
> *integration, selfless action, and unity of purpose rarely*
> *achieved in human history.*[7]

We elevate ourselves and people around us by overcoming ego, materialism, prejudices, and disunity. Rather than waiting for someone else to rescue us, ultimately we must save ourselves. We will become heroes.

In our private moments, we can turn to a Higher Power through prayer and meditation as we seek assistance and courage. In our communities, we can associate with others who share our values. The Bahá'í community, with believers literally throughout the world, is working in parallel to improve communities and to prepare the future generation for its role.

And finally, we can enlarge our vision to embrace the world and align our deeds with the best interests of humanity and our planet. In other words, we can orient ourselves toward being heroes every day. In the words of 'Abdu'l-Bahá:

> . . . become the light of the world, the soul for the body of the world, the comfort and help for humanity, and the source of salvation for the whole universe.[8]

The stories about how we do this would not make a fun movie. The action might not even be visible, especially in the absence of explosions, fights, or chase scenes. We aren't wearing capes or masks or doing any fancy martial arts. Yet in the absence of cameras, possibly without an audience, here we are. Doing what we can to help others and to create a better future.

4. Prosperity: More Than Wealth

Hoping to better organize my home office, I got an additional bookcase this week. Among the books I can readily see again are several on the theme of prosperity. Much like greeting old friends, I spent some time flipping through them, re-acquainting myself with their ideas. Through a range of perspectives and authors, they explore interrelated concepts including prosperity, abundance, success, and contentment.

For many years, beginning before I became a Bahá'í, I have been intrigued with the concept of prosperity. Conceptually it is intangible and reaches beyond the material. Surely prosperity is not about so-much-money or status or a luxurious life. Linked to the concepts of plenty and abundance, it is self-defined rather than quantified by others. As a spiritual condition, it transcends (though perhaps incorporates) the material state.

One of the best definitions I've ever seen of the word "prosperity" is on the first page of a book by Catherine Ponder, a minister within the Unity Church:

> *You are prosperous to the degree that you are experiencing peace, health, and plenty in your world.*[9]

Mahatma Gandhi defined it this way:

> *It is health that is real wealth and not pieces of gold and silver.*[10]

The idea of both prosperity and material wealth is discussed in almost all religious and faith traditions. Sometimes it is written within a prayer asking for abundance; sometimes it is an acknowledgement of sufficiency. Prosperity is often related to peace, to strong character, to education, to honorable living. Many speak of God as the source, and they also remind us of the responsibilities that come with it.

Recognizing prosperity as a spiritual state does not mean that we shouldn't be concerned with material prosperity. Life is practical, and the desire to live more comfortably is consistent with being thankful at times of need. Our planet and its beauty have been created for us to enjoy and to enhance. And since this requires material assets then acquiring those assets can be a worthy goal. Key to this, however, is doing so with gratitude and appreciation, without being driven by materialism or seeking social status.

The Bahá'í Writings explore the sources of material sufficiency and even state that a mature society requires more than sufficiency, i.e. wealth. Foremost among the sources of these material resources is work, whether that is through a profession, crafts, or a host of other endeavors. Income generated through work provides the means for our own maintenance and a more secure future.

The Writings also encourage generosity in times of prosperity. They tell us to be grateful for that prosperity, even while recognizing it as a temporary state. As such, we should also be thankful during times of shortage or insufficiency, since that condition brings its own lessons and may also pass away.

Beyond our own personal interests, 'Abdu'l-Bahá wrote that broadening our thinking can bring about material prosperity, even at a global scale. Describing the progress of a person from concern for self to the family, community, and country, he concluded:

> . . . . when ideas and views reach the utmost degree of expansion and . . . perfection, then will he be interested in the exaltation of humankind . . . the well-wisher of all men and the seeker of the weal and prosperity of all lands.[11]

The prevailing focus on materialism and self-interest can be overcome with increased concern for all humanity. Together we can choose to think about universal prosperity and base our actions on that as a primary concern. Everyone is worthy of health and sufficiency; all deserve abundance. And we all crave perfection.

5. A Change of Pace

I happened to overhear a young woman in a coffee shop tell a friend that she had just seen a classic Western movie. She was disappointed to find that it didn't have the same level of action and the fast pace of today's films. In sum: not enough adrenaline rush.

Though she probably overgeneralized the pace of older films compared to newer ones, I agree with her observation if I apply that trend to daily life. It does seem now that almost everything occurs at an accelerating pace.

People can say this is subjective, that a minute is still a minute, a day is still a day. But quantity and quality are not the same thing. Even if the measurement of time is the same, we experience life as getting faster, more intense, or both.

As a Bahá'í, I attribute this to the coming of Bahá'u'lláh — both the nature and the magnitude of His Message. The past 150 years have been characterized by the breaking down of institutions concurrently with the creation of new ones. Recent generations have seen an acceleration of this rate of change, and we now have the means to know about events even as they are occurring anywhere on the planet.

If we could travel back to the time of previous Messengers, we would find that each brought teachings that changed the fundamentals of their time and place. One of the distinguishing principles brought by Bahá'u'lláh is unity. We are even now seeing reverberations due to the shift from disunity to unity. Admittedly distressing to watch and experience, it is inevitable and is taking us to a better world.

'Abdu'l-Bahá gave this explanation:

> *Mankind needs a universal motive power to quicken it.*
> *The inspired messenger who is directly assisted by the*
> *power of God brings about universal results.*[12]

Comparing this to the physical world, he also said:

The light and heat of the sun cause the earth to be fruitful, and create life in all things that grow; and the Holy Spirit quickens the souls of men.[13]

The word "quickens" has many meanings, and somehow they all seem to describe today's fast pace. Among its definitions are concepts such as vitalizing and stimulating. Today's world seems to be more alive due to new potentialities.

We know that both growth and change are intrinsic to life. This is nothing new, and it will never end. But now, beyond the turning of seasons and the natural urge to grow, beyond the physical and material explanations that we might otherwise offer, we can sense a new impetus propelling us forward.

As reflected in action films and novels, reported in print media, demonstrated through broadcast news media, and accessed through the Internet and the Web — our world is changing rapidly. These changes in turn challenge our ability to change with it.

It might be timely and even valuable to discuss with a friend, perhaps at a coffee shop, how prepared we are to respond to the current pace of living. We might ask questions like: How adaptable am I? What are my resources? How wide are my perspectives? How trusting am I in the results? Do I have a larger vision for the future? Am I aligned with other like-minded people? Am I riding the waves or struggling against the current? Questions this complex require more than a cup of coffee. A refill and muffin would help.

6. Connecting with Science and Art

Sorting papers in my office this morning, I opened a file with stories collected over the years from print magazines such as *Newsweek*. Rereading some of them, I was particularly amused by a story in which pianist Jeremy Denk wrote about his own "My Favorite Mistake"[14] — trying to major in both chemistry and music. He had been attracted to both, thinking they would be complementary, and seeing within them the virtues (his word) of consistency, repeatability, calm precision, and rhythm.

Alas it didn't work out for him, as he ended up at the bottom of the class in chemistry. It seems the differences between the two just didn't suit him academically. His greatest difficulty was a desire for innovation and improvisation, which could be dangerous in a chemistry lab, especially in the hands of a novice. And then there was the matter of levels of precision, i.e. in chemistry there is often just a single right answer, while in music he saw infinite possibilities.

I love this story, because it so beautifully illustrates the balance between science and art, which in turn is similar to the balance between science and religion. Mr. Denk eventually resolved the tension between the two for himself, just as most of us are probably more inclined one way or the other. The important thing is not to become focused on one at the exclusion of the other.

Reflecting on the emphasis in the Bahá'í Faith on pursuing both art and science, I did a word search through an electronic version of the Writings and found that more often than not a hit on the word "arts" pointed not just to that word but also to the phrase "arts and science." So while we may not be adept at both, many of the qualities within one mirror and complement the qualities in the other.

Leonardo da Vinci saw the connection between the two. He has been quoted as saying:

> *Principles for the Development of a Complete Mind:*
> *Study the science of art. Study the art of science. Develop*
> *your senses, especially learn how to see. Realize that*
> *everything connects to everything else.*[15]

There is a practical side to this, too. An artist, like a scientist, must know his/her materials and supplies. And if he wants to be a professional, then he must practice self-discipline and adopt sound business practices. Similarly, a scientist who wants to advance professionally will want to explore and to innovate. Considering the attributes of a balanced person, we benefit from being at least somewhat involved in both — for example a scientist with a music collection or a potter who collects and studies fossils.

On a higher level, 'Abdu'l-Bahá considered the study of science and art as part of the foundation for education and wrote that proficiency in them can be considered worship. In his words:

> *Sciences and arts, industry and invention have been*
> *reformed. Law and ethics have been reconstituted,*
> *reorganized. The world of thought has been regenerated.*
> *. . Present exigencies demand new methods of solution;*
> *world problems are without precedent. Old ideas and*
> *modes of thought are fast becoming obsolete.*[16]

I don't think it's any accident that the past century has seen great acceleration of both science and art. Having been inspired to advance, they vibrate with new possibilities. Hardly a week goes by without news about science, medicine, or technology. And the same is true with the arts, especially if we consider the full range of arts and how they have been leveraged through technology. Indeed, it's getting difficult to differentiate between the two.

The importance of the arts and science was also affirmed by the United Nations through this statement within *The Universal Declaration of Human Rights:*

> *Everyone has the right freely to participate in the cultural life of the community, to enjoy the arts and to share in scientific advancement and its benefits.*[17]

When I look at the world around me, and when I consider how much I enjoy through both science and the arts, I am reminded of how fortunate I am. Science has contributed to my healthy life, and arts keep me enriched. Our challenge now is to ensure that both advance responsibly, are uplifting, and are universally accessible.

7. Surrounded by Beauty

Odd as this may sound, I love movies about prisoners of war (POWs). I am always inspired by stories that show people arising above unfathomably horrid circumstances. As these films show, this can include POWs, who somehow managed to maintain dignity, establish bonds of friendship, and create something that felt like home.

I recently watched a film that vividly showed the extent to which the POWs strive to create beauty in their barracks; surely the need to be surrounded by beauty is a fundamental human trait. Ever since watching that film, I've been thinking more about beauty as a universal concept.

We notice beauty in nature, such as a waterfall or a sunset. We create it from natural materials, perhaps as a floral arrangement or a well-planned garden. We design and build it, whether the result is major architecture or a backyard shed. We express it through our own talents, such as in music or cooking.

Beauty can also be recognized within true human progress. As 'Abdu'l-Bahá indicated:

> . . . when divers shades of thought, temperament and
> character are brought together, the beauty and glory of
> human perfection will be revealed and made manifest.[18]

Accordingly, we are encouraged to promote beauty, whether natural or man-made, as a guiding principle in community planning. We also want to surround ourselves with beauty in our homes and daily lives.

The concept of beauty is prominent within the Bahá'í Faith. As just one indication of this, Bahá'u'lláh is often referred to as "The Blessed Beauty." So what does beauty here in this world do for us other than delight our senses? In a profound way, it can touch the heart and inspire us to noble sentiments and actions.

There is beauty in creativity and innovation. For example, I have seen videos by the Vienna Vegetable Orchestra. The members of this group make their own musical instruments daily from fresh fruits and vegetables. I find the idea itself so innovative and charming that, regardless of anyone's personal taste in music, truly the orchestra members have created beauty.

There is beauty in human concord and peace. When we put pointless, wasteful prejudices aside, we discover that we are one in service to humanity. Much like birds that differ in outward form or color, we can learn to live together in peace and to love each other. Requisite to this is recognizing the beauty in all people by shifting our gaze from external beauty to beauty within, to value above all a person's substance, character, and personality.

Subtler forms of beauty can be a friendly smile or a kindly deed. Every one of us can surround ourselves with — and extend to others — these simple, deeply satisfying instances of beauty. If POWs can create beauty in their surroundings, how much more can the rest of us do.

8. At a Magic Show

I recently attended an event featuring a magician. Most of the time he focused his attention on the children, inviting them to participate in some of his tricks. At some point I found myself looking at the audience and not at him, and I noticed that all ages were captivated by his magic as well as his banter.

I also noticed that the children were impressed with the wow-ooh-ahh of it all, while the adults were in the how-did-he-do-that mode. Reflecting on this, I think that both reactions are desirable.

The children are representative of the part of us that lives in the moment. Characterized by feeling, they see wonder in nature, don't overanalyze, and accept that not everything can be explained in terms they can presently understand. I will label this *faith*.

The adults are representative of the part of us that seeks understanding and control. Characterized by thinking, we ask questions, we value science and process, and we seek evidence or even proof. I will label this *reason*.

Of course, not all children think one way, just as not all adults behave another way. As people in a variety of circumstances, we are a mixture of both. This demonstrates the Bahá'í principle of the essential agreement between religion and science. Sadly, history offers ample evidence of the conflict and disunity that can result from an imbalance between these two key areas of thought and practice. Even today, many people believe that there is some basic opposition between science and religion, that one contradicts the other on some points, and that we must choose between being a religious person (a believer in God) or a scientist (a follower of reason).

On the other hand, both have a place in our lives, and both are subject to change or at least re-interpretation. What science can explain and how we understand and apply it — this changes over time. Yesterday's mysteries, once solved, can be quite ordinary. Indeed, we are surrounded by items that would have been unfathomable in times past.

If we regard science and religion in a balanced way, we find the harmony between them. Danger comes from taking either one to its extreme. More specifically, if religious beliefs and opinions are found contrary to the standards of science then they are superstitions, the result of imagination, or unfounded ritual. The reverse is true as well; just because something can't be proved or explained does not mean it is not true. This is where faith comes into the picture. As 'Abdu'l-Bahá said:

> *Religion and Science are inter-twined with each other*
> *and cannot be separated. These are the two wings with*
> *which humanity must fly. One wing is not enough.*[19]

As scientific enquiry advances so must our ideas be open to testing and to reshaping. I do not need science to explain everything. Rather, God (or whatever name one may prefer) is unknowable. This doesn't scare or alarm me; I accept that as a given.

I continue to be curious about the nature of the universe. For example, I want to know about life on other planets. I am also comforted that others with specific expertise are learning how to prevent floods in SE Asia, how to sanitize water in Africa, how to eliminate or manage diseases, and ever so much more. I don't need to know everything myself, since humanity is increasingly taking a global approach to applying science to problems around the world.

Similarly, I don't need to know how the magician made the rings interlock, how the card jumped from one child's hand to another, or even how the rabbit fitted into his hat and later turned into a dove. I can enjoy the show and join the children in the wonder of it all.

9. Poverty in a Bottle

I am currently involved in a project called "making poverty history." In the process of working on it, I have been investigating the causes of poverty. The film *The Gods Must Be Crazy*[20] is as insightful today as when it was made in 1980; and it offers at least some of the explanation.

In this film, a community of Kalahari Bushmen is thrown off-balance when a Coke bottle is tossed out of a small plane and lands in their village. Before that moment, everyone had everything they needed; they knew how to live in their own environment and with each other. But suddenly there was a Coke bottle, something they had never seen before and frankly didn't know what to do with.

Thinking it a gift from the gods, they found that it could be handy. Gradually it changed from novelty to toy to tool and even to a weapon. And, since there was only one Coke bottle, for the first time they experienced lack, unfairness, deprivation. They soon became a community with "haves" and "have-nots"; they were no longer content.

Drawing on the metaphor from this film, it seems that we now have a world in which too many people lack Coke bottles. There are enough Coke bottles in existence; there are just too many in some places and not enough in others.

I recognize that individual circumstances, choices, and talents will result in a range of lifestyles. My concern here is with extremes of poverty and wealth. A world with homelessness and hunger, with wars started over a patch of land or a trickle of water — these are symptoms of extreme imbalance, immoderation, and injustice.

The Coke bottles in today's world are not fairly distributed because of the absence of worldwide agreement, which itself stems from disunity. Instead, we have prejudices and greed. Thus, people are prevented from helping themselves, from helping neighbors, and from helping nameless strangers.

Poverty is a global phenomenon, including in the so-called "developed world." From homelessness in cities and towns across the country to unemployed suburbanites, no place is exempt.

In less-developed parts of our world, people are capable and resourceful, but the obstacles to their economic development are vast. Surely we want to help them overcome these barriers through sharing of knowledge and resources.

Most approaches to solving poverty emphasize factors such as geography, politics, distribution logistics, and economics. I agree that on a practical level these challenges must be solved, but they don't get to the source of the extremes of poverty and wealth — unless they are guided by a concern for justice.

Writing about root causes and permanent solutions to poverty, the Bahá'í International Community stated:

> *The economic relationships of a society reflect the values*
> *of its members . . . Until justice is valued over greed, the*
> *gap between the rich and the poor will continue to widen,*
> *and the dream of sustainable economic growth, peace*
> *and prosperity will elude our grasp.*[21]

On a personal level, every individual can help to create a world with increased unity of vision, where justice and fairness — rather than cold economics, short-term solutions, or materialistic self-interest — are the bases for policy. We can do this through being informed, engaged in activities directed toward these goals, and sharing our own material resources.

I have read about many items and methods that cost very little (relative to today's Western standards) yet can accomplish so much. For example: a straw-like device that allows individuals to filter their own drinking water; and bed-sized mosquito netting to reduce exposure to malaria (which threatens more lives than HIV/AIDS in many places). Both offer long-term benefits and cost about the same as a single lunch at a mid-range restaurant in the US or Canada.

If I believe that we are all one human family, then other people's poverty is my problem, too. Its pervasiveness is a reminder to think and think again. Do I need this or that item or could I give more generously to charity? Do I buy items that benefit the person who made or grew it?

As yet one more reminder to think beyond my own immediate surroundings, I can consider this quote from Charles Dickens. In his encouragement to extend the idea of charity to the level of justice, he reminds us to think beyond ourselves::

Charity begins at home, and justice begins next door. [22]

I feel fortunate that I am not myself living in poverty. Being conscious of my own habits is one step. Another step is to realize that having the means for daily living also means having enough to share — lovingly, consciously, and consistently.

10. The Talent Within Us All

Like many gyms, the one I go do has large TVs in front of the cardio equipment. It passes the time nicely, and over the years I have seen countless segments of old sitcoms, movies, talk shows, and much more. This afternoon, I happened to notice that several channels were showing talent competitions. Not just for entertainment, these were contests wherein there would be one winner and everyone else would be a loser.

Two ideas immediately struck me. Firstly, there are many immensely talented people around. Secondly, most of them were going to lose.

OK, I understand that someone-somewhere needs to decide what to put on the air, so judging is inherent in this type of broadcasting. And the "losers" might benefit from the exposure gained from being on the program in the first place. On the other hand, who can possibly say who is the most talented? I would not want to be in that position.

In the past, the word "talent" was used for money, too. Perhaps the most familiar instance is the Bible's Parable of the Talents[23] in which talents as currency were both a reward and a means for investment. Bringing this to modern times, what if we valued our collective wealth as the sum of everyone's talents? What if we sought to increase our wealth by recognizing and developing those talents?

As 'Abdu'l-Bahá said, referring to our Creator:

> *Thou hast provided for all, conferrest life upon all, hast endowed each and all with talents and faculties.*[24]

Since everyone has talents, we can see these as including more than performance arts. Some people have a talent for cooking, organizing, gardening, comforting others, fixing things — well, just about anything we can think of.

Recognizing the value of bringing out the innate capacities of all people, Shoghi Effendi encouraged organizations to:

> ...capitalize the talents of all the members of the group and keep them busy in some form of active participation.[25]

The scope of this vision is so large that elsewhere it is written that the moral character of civilization itself depends on people using both their brains and their talents. In the future we will accept the oneness of humanity and welcome the full spectrum of capacities and talents. Rather than seeking uniformity, we will cherish a wide range of experiences, cultures, and viewpoints; together they contribute to the human family's progress and well-being.

It seems to me that we have a duty to provide an opportunity for everyone to develop their talents and channel them in a constructive way. This includes linking them to professions, hobbies, and other such fruitful endeavors.

I love being entertained as much as anyone else — music, theatre, film, arts, pop culture — and I may watch some of those talent competitions on TV. Beyond that, I want to appreciate the talents in everyone without being tempted to evaluate or judge. If no one needs to lose then surely we all win.

II. Living in the Present

I often read books and watch films that can be called "dystopian." While asking provocative questions, they typically portray the future as a dark, troubled place. Less common are books and films that compare the present with the past. A highly entertaining film that does just that is Woody Allen's *Midnight in Paris*[26] It asks us to consider whether earlier times were better than the present.

Or is it just a longing for a *different* time? If not an earlier time, then would living in the future be better? Or is this whole thing just another example of the cliché "the grass is always greener on the other side of the fence"? Perhaps it is merely a symptom of discontent.

What is contentment anyway? We often think of it as being a feeling of physical comfort and ease. After a busy day we sit back, relax, and sigh with contentment.

We know that animals are content when their physical needs are met. They don't pass judgment about time or place. They live and even prosper when they have enough food, water, an ambient temperature, and a satisfactory social structure.

As physical beings we have much in common with animals, yet we are vastly more. We have powers of thought and free will far beyond the comprehension of animals. These words from 'Abdu'l-Bahá enlarge this idea:

> *How can man be content to lead only an animal existence when God has made him so high a creature? . . . But to man God has given such wonderful power that he can guide, control and overcome nature.*[27]

This power comes with great responsibilities, which are mitigated through our also being spiritual beings. As such, a moral conscience guides and limits us, telling us to look for the greater good in our deeds. And since nothing happens in isolation, we consider our impact on the planet and other people. In contrast to animals, which simply act according to the fixed laws of nature, we contribute through our work. Because this comes through free will, it is another source of contentment and satisfaction.

We also feel content when we are secure within a supportive social environment. Having a loving family, loyal friends, congenial neighbors, and cooperative colleagues can bring joy and contentment, even when other circumstances are difficult.

If we extend our thinking about this social environment to the community, then we can be content when we trust that other people are taking care of the essentials. Living in a well-organized society where all residents can depend on infrastructure and continuity of governance is a great blessing. Far from taking these things for granted, I am grateful for being relieved of daily worries about items such as clean water and dependable power supplies.

Contentment in harsh circumstances can be learned from Bahá'u'lláh and 'Abdu'l-Bahá, both of whom were long-time prisoners in some of the harshest prisons in the world. Yet they both wrote that even in those circumstances they were happy and content. They had transcended the physical and were connected to higher realms.

Paraphrasing a passage from Bahá'u'lláh's book *The Seven Valleys*, Adib Taherzadeh wrote:

> *Only those who have entered the valley of contentment have experienced true joy, even though their lives be subjected to affliction and suffering.*[28]

There is a lesson in this as well — including that each of us is where and when we need to be, and we have choices about how we regard our lives here and now.

Every place and time have their own challenges and needs, and this is where contentment needs to be separated from complacency. Being content does not mean we should be lulled into complacency. To the contrary, contentment can be the launching point, allowing movement from strength to strength. Being content and happy with where and when I am living allows me to be actively engaged in improving my character and contributing to the advancement of society.

Dwelling in nostalgia can be distracting. It is better to learn from the past and apply those lessons. Likewise, if I look so far into the future that I become removed from the present then I will miss opportunities here and now. It is better to have a goal in mind and work toward it.

If I do this, then the answer to the question "Was the past better?" is "no" — and the question "Will the future be better?" gets a confident "yes."

Chapter 6
Nature and the Environment

1. Nutrients for the Future

Hiking through a regional park on a lovely summer day, I paused to read a sign along an interpretative trail. It told the story of a devastating storm that resulted in the falling of many of the forest's giant trees. The message ended with:

> *They will be left here to provide nutrients for the next*
> *generation of giants.*[1]

Storms, fires, earthquakes — these are some of nature's tools for regenerating. From a human perspective, these are dramatic and traumatic events, though we recognize them as both natural and cyclical. As in the forest I was visiting, each generation leaves a legacy for the next. That in turn becomes its nourishment.

As I considered the scale of that storm and the geological timeframe in which this sort of event occurs, I wondered about these ideas in the social sense. We live in communities with commerce and cultural sharing. What feeds us now? What nutrients are we leaving for future generations? Who will be the giants?

First on my list of what feeds us is belief in the future. Children eventually think beyond their Halloween costume and want to "be" something when they grow up. We have ideas about how we want to live, experiences we want to have, and how we want to engage with others. Of course, not all of this will come true, as life will offer its surprises as well as disappointments. But looking forward is inspiring and motivates us to dream, plan, and act.

Education, science, and the arts feed us. To learn is to live, and science is more than a means to better technologies and comforts. It is also a means to observe and realize the wonders of life itself. Similarly, the arts are more than home decorating, entertainment, and fashion. True art also heightens our imaginations and leaves us considering new possibilities.

If we are to bundle these ideas into nutrients for the future, then they should contribute to a peaceful civilization and a healthier planet. That time will also be characterized by freedom from prejudice, equality of men and women, elimination of extremes of poverty and wealth, and abandonment of partisan interests. Concern for the welfare of all will be paramount.

Describing the physical relationship of mankind, 'Abdu'l-Bahá tells us:

> *Human brotherhood and dependence exist because mutual helpfulness and cooperation are the two necessary principles underlying human welfare.*[2]

Relating this to the metaphor of nutrient, we will want to ensure that no one is hungry, homeless, ill, or despairing. We will build systems and safeguards for all, and geographic boundaries will not stop us from caring. Rather, these boundaries will invite new ways to cooperate and reciprocate.

I don't know who will be considered giants — heroes — in the future. Presently they are often youthful billionaires, business innovators, athletes, pop culture stars, and others known at a public level. And yes, there are also lesser-known philanthropists and others who perform great deeds. But I'm wondering if a future, properly nourished world will be a more generous and loving place.

How far into the future dare we look? If we were to compare ourselves to a generation ago, are we better off? So what might be the situation five generations from now? What about 10 generations? Or even more?

The Bahá'í International Community in the 1999 document *Who Is Writing the Future* stated:

However great the turmoil, the period into which humanity is moving will open to every individual, every institution, and every community on earth unprecedented opportunities to participate in the writing of the planet's future.[3]

A forest regenerates slowly, while our human time frame is swifter. If we're going to believe in the future, we need to recognize that our own actions — now — are the nutrients for the future. Let's feed it well.

2. Shades of Grey

I pulled up the window shades this morning, but the room didn't get any brighter. Yuck, it's one of those days when the world looks like an old, faded black & white photograph. At first glance, it seemed to be a blah day, colorless, drab, even depressing.

And then I thought about black & white photographs taken by Ansel Adams and other great photographers. The shades of grey are beautiful and stirring, since in the absence of color we see shadows and new depths.

Ansel Adams, sharing his own thoughts about art and creativity and their role in helping us make sense of the world, said:

> *In wisdom gathered over time I have found that every experience is a form of exploration.*[4]

In many respects, this is how the world works. More than being just black and white, much of life is shades of grey — subject to exploration and interpretation, influenced by context, and located somewhere along a continuum.

A few weeks ago, a doctor of Chinese Medicine prescribed a herbal remedy that prepares the body for the winter season. She told me to start taking it on the 1st day of the winter according to the lunar calendar. Even the seasons can be determined in relative terms.

The same thing goes for holidays. New Year is not a fixed date around the world. As a Bahá'í I observe the New Year on the 1st day of spring in the Northern Hemisphere. March 21st is the New Year within many countries including Iran and Afghanistan. In my childhood (Jewish) home, we observed the New Year in September, on a date that varied with the lunar calendar. The Chinese New Year is in February. In Thailand it is the 13th of April. For the Hmong people the date shifts slightly from year to year, depending on the condition of the rice harvest.

Likewise, many of our actions (and reactions to others' actions) are conditioned by our own cultural standards. For example, I consider punctuality to be a sign of courtesy, respect, trustworthiness, and integrity. Yet this is not true everywhere. In some places, being on time for a dinner party would mean catching the hosts unprepared, as they would never expect people to be on time and might even consider their punctual guests to be rude. And in some places travel is so difficult that punctuality means arriving as agreed — plus or minus a couple of days.

This "shades of grey" concept can be applied in other areas of life. Rather than being considered smart or not-smart, children could be evaluated based on whether they are living up to their own potential. An athletic team isn't just a winner or a loser but rather is a social group that played well together or could be improved. A person isn't fat/thin, tall/short, strong/weak, pretty/plain but rather is someone who takes care of himself and is well-groomed.

Ageism is common in North America. Yet in the Orient and to Native peoples age is thought to bring wisdom and is both respected and cherished. (The older I get, the more I hope this is true!)

Social conditions vary in both time and place — as does the degree of awareness and concern of the people themselves. One of the underpinning of the Bahá'í Faith is the distinction between spiritual and social teachings. On one hand, some truths (teachings) are constant, unchanging, and present in all world religions; on the other hand, social teachings change and progress to address the issues of the times. The interplay between these two (absolute and relative) truths guides elements of human life as we evolve an increasing level of spiritual maturity and social consciousness.

And some exceptionally difficult issues face us all right now. For example, climate change has the potential to change the very geography of our planet. Proposed solutions include technological approaches, political interventions, and social changes. Some people question to what extent we should try to intervene, based on economic (financial) grounds. It seems to me that, if environmental issues were to be considered through the lens of spiritual or moral standards, then suitable action could be agreed upon.

In the physical world, sunshine helps us to see objects in their full color. And then when we look out of the window we realize that some things actually are grey, while others are bright and colorful. In a similar way, through the light of spiritual truths and moral principles we can see the spectrum of human diversity as we work together for the benefit of all.

3. Seasons and Cycles

I spent two hours today raking and mulching leaves — for the fourth time this fall. Despite the work required for cleanup chores, I feel fortunate to have so many mature, beautiful trees in my own yard and throughout the neighborhood.

As a child I played in the leaves. And then when the playtime ended, my parents would burn them. We didn't know about the environmental impact of this practice; that's just the way things were done then.

I have lived in places without physically obvious seasons yet with other landmarks throughout the year such as holidays or the first day of school. Whether we mark the seasons by the weather or by events, we humans note the passage and cycles of time.

Around here, fall is more than just a messy time of the year. It is also a time for completing outdoor projects and preparing for what's next. Squirrels busily store food, and I clean up my yard from the summer's activities.

Winter is a time for a slower pace and at-home projects, with a quiet that seems to infuse nature. And while outdoor sports and games do exist, the cold tends to keep me indoors for longer periods of time.

Probably nothing is more welcome than the signs of spring. As soon as bulbs appear through the snow, people seem to be in a happier mood. Longer days of light recharge our energy, and hope is in the air. It is a time for rebirth in nature, a time for celebration.

And then we have summer with its sunshine, heat, energy, and so many possibilities for enjoyment. Children and youth are away from school and might have different arenas for learning or seasonal jobs.

Reflecting on the idea that everything in life has its parallel in the spiritual world and that seasons represent cycles of life itself, I came across this quotation from 'Abdu'l-Bahá:

In this material world time has cycles; places change through alternating seasons, and for souls there are progress, retrogression and education. . .[5]

The well-known passage from the Book of Ecclesiastes underscores not only the reality of seasons but also that everything has its time:

To every thing there is a season, and a time to every purpose under the heaven.[6]

If a physical year has seasons and if every thing has its time, then even spiritual practice (religion) has its seasons and cycles. 'Abdu'l-Bahá referred to the Bahá'í Faith as bringing a spiritual springtime through its principles, practices, and institutions:

Now the new age is here and creation is reborn. Humanity hath taken on new life. . . and the reviving spring is here. All things are now made new. Arts and industries have been reborn, there are new discoveries in science, and there are new inventions . . . Renewal is the order of the day.[7]

Depending on where we live, the physical experience of the seasons will differ. Regardless of these variations, in our daily lives we are aware of changes in our physical environment. Changes in the spiritual climate may be subtler, but they are real. Even though we know that our world is experiencing serious problems, we also perceive indications of a new spirit of optimism, dignity, faith, and well-being.

It doesn't happen at the same rate everywhere, and progress doesn't have linear forward movement. But overall we have reason to be hopeful. Whatever the calendar may say, we are in a period of renewal. Much like a bulb appearing through the snow, we ourselves are living in a time of transition — with better weather and better times ahead.

4. Better Than Gold

A few years ago, I lost my gold wedding ring under odd circumstances. I was in a friend's car when a sudden movement of my hand resulted in it flying off my finger. We both saw it happen, and we both leaned forward to retrieve it from the floor. But it wasn't there. It had vanished!

Weird as that was, almost as odd is that she contacted me this morning to tell me that she found it. It had somehow lodged itself in a previously undetected pocket under the seat. After such a long time without it, when I put in on again I had an emotional reaction, akin to a sense of reunion.

I've heard stories from other people who have sentimental ties to gold jewelry received as gifts from their spouses, parents, or grandparents. What is it about gold as a symbol as well as a substance that evokes such reactions?

It's not that gold is rare, though mining requires a lot of work. Nor is it innately beautiful, as anyone who has seen it in its natural state knows; intense heat is required to bring out its beauty. From a practical standpoint, it is desirably for jewelry, sculpture, and even dentistry due to its malleability. But more than a raw material for crafts, gold figures prominently within other arenas — both concrete and abstract.

For many years, the financial world measured currencies against it, hence the term "gold standard." And though this is no longer common practice, the phrase persists as an idiom for a widely accepted measure of value and quality.

In mathematics, architecture, and the arts the term "golden ratio" refers to proportions generally considered aesthetically pleasing.

In philosophy, we read about the "golden mean" as a desirable midpoint between extremes. Similar to "the middle way," this idea is especially associated with Confucius.

Researching how gold is mentioned within religious traditions, I found this quotation from 'Abdu'l-Bahá. It touches on the metaphor of our being tested and improved through the heat of tests:

> *So too will solid gold wondrously gleam and shine out in the assayer's fire. It is clear, then, that tests and trials are, for sanctified souls, but God's bounty and grace . . .*[8]

And of course there is the "golden rule" and its counterpart in most (if not all) religious traditions. Though the label itself is usually associated with the Christian version, its origins go to the earliest known religions. As such it is a spiritual truth, unchangeable throughout time, universal in its application — as differentiated from social teachings, which evolve over time.

With gold already meaning so much to us, I am thinking about yet another phrase that mentions it: "Golden Age."

The Golden Age, as promised by Bahá'u'lláh, will be a time when humanity will realize its potential, people will live in love and harmony, and the planet itself will be cherished and healthy. And though this age is far off in the future, Bahá'u'lláh tells us that we all have a part to play in bringing it to reality. Furthermore, He links our individual efforts to create the future world with the very purpose of our existence. In His words:

> *All men have been created to carry forward an ever-advancing civilization.*[9]

This motivates me to ensure that my own actions are guided by spiritual principles such as love for humanity and for our planet. And I am inspired to know that if my actions are loving, my character improved through tests, my actions responsible, my vision turned toward unity, then that's good as — even better than — gold.

5. It's Sunny Where I Live

Every morning I check the weather forecast — not only for the current day but also for future days. Depending on the prediction, I might change my plans, my clothes, or both. So for me, there's no such thing as bad weather, just weather I didn't get ready for.

I originally adopted that attitude many years ago while living in the Pacific Northwest. I found that if I waited for good weather then many things simply wouldn't happen. So I learned to buy coats with hoods and to be flexible in my planning. As a result, I had many experiences that were fun, educational, or entertaining — perhaps especially so because they were not as originally expected.

Weather is a suitable metaphor for the conditions in which I am living. If I adopt that as my overall approach to life, then things not going the way I might have wished becomes a signal to put aside my disappointment and accept that something better is happening instead. Even if I can't yet see the outcome.

As written by Bahá'u'lláh:

> *The source of all glory is acceptance of whatsoever the Lord hath bestowed, and contentment with that which God hath ordained.*[10]

I'm not sure that going to a museum rather than a picnic elevates me to the level of glory, but the point is to learn detachment from my own preconceived notions. And by practicing on the little things then I will be better prepared when bigger things occur.

And they will occur. Life always presents us with surprises, opportunities to grow, and a chance to reflect on what has happened. Even if sometimes it seems that the storms of life will never pass, they do.

So how can I prepare for storms? In the physical world I can close windows, turn up the heat, put on suitable clothes, buy insurance, repair leaks, keep emergency supplies within easy reach, coordinate mutual assistance with neighbors, and take other such measures.

Within myself I can prepare by having faith in the greater good, meditating and praying, maintaining supportive relationships, and integrating inner strength gained through earlier events. Having gotten through difficulties in the past helps me to get through present ones. Recognizing the extent of my present capabilities gives me confidence to face the future. And having confidence in myself puts me in a better position to help others, just as sometimes I am the one who needs help.

I can also be thankful for the weather, good or bad. And for that matter, I can quit using labels like "good" or "bad" and instead consider it "sunny" if I am ready for it. Even if that isn't literally true, it is another day, another incident in life, and another learning experience.

Being grateful for every day is a sign of spiritual maturity. Thinking back to my years in the Pacific Northwest, there is much to be thankful for. The landscape is green most of the year, both the ocean and mountains are nearby, people are friendly, the food is fresh, and the coffee is tasty. Life is good.

Spiritual maturity is shown through how we behave in sunshine as well as in storms. This can happen through such simple and daily acts as being happy, sharing prosperity, being kind to strangers, greeting everyone with a warm smile, and offering friendly words.

We may not know it at the time, but the stranger who receives our kindness, the person who sees our smile — that may be someone in the midst of their own private storm. Sharing our own sunshine might help them get through their day, especially if they weren't prepared for it.

6. Salt, Not Just for Food

I went out for lunch with a friend today, and as she added salt to her soup she offered this quotation from Isak Dinesen:

> *The cure for anything is salt water: sweat, tears or the sea.*[11]

We shared a smile at the cleverness of this quote and then resumed our own conversation. Now, a few hours later, I am thinking about salt being more than an ingredient in food or useful in food preservation.

To begin with the obvious, salt is part of our natural environment. Present in our body cells and in most living tissues, it is so essential to life that entire cities and economies have been developed around it. It served as a chief factor in trade, transportation systems, the building of empires, and even wars.

The quotation begins with salt's role in healing, starting with the salt in our own sweat. Inducing sweat is a well-accepted health practice, such as in a sauna or a ceremonial sweat lodge. And then there is sweat through physical labor or daily living. Even if my job doesn't literally make me sweat, I do feel refreshed and invigorated when I work hard and produce results.

To consider the second part of the quotation, what about tears? Well, science tells us that we release toxins through tears, and on that basis we can say that tears are healing. Crying is also a way of showing that we care. This is true in both good and not-so-good times and when we are emotionally stirred, such as through music, a sunset, or thrilling news.

The quotation concludes with the sea. Commercially sold sea salts are called "designer salt" by many people, akin to snake oil. Yet these salts are part of many people's regular health regime. For example, Dead Sea mud is used for health treatments by people who believe that the specific concentration of mineral salts has healing powers. Beyond these admittedly debatable examples, we do know that the movement of the tides, the ebb and flow of the sea, and the negative ions released by this movement have a soothing effect.

The sea appears prominently in literature and the arts, often metaphorically. Within the Bahá'í Writings are many passages comparing the sea to humanity. Just to list a few from 'Abdu'l-Bahá:

> *The sea of the unity of mankind is lifting up its waves with joy. . .*
>
> *You are all waves of one sea, mirrors of one reflection.*
>
> *All mankind will dwell together as one family, blend as the waves of one sea, shine as stars of one firmament and appear as fruits of the same tree.*[12]

Returning to Dinesen's quotation, in these instances salt is essential and possibly a cure. But this is only true if it is present in a moderate amount. Too much salt in our diets contributes to cardiovascular disease, while not enough can lead to dehydration and even death. We want to work, but not too much. We are enriched by our emotions, though we don't want to be overwhelmed. We depend on the seas but are threatened by floods and tsunamis.

Salt is not rare. Nevertheless, like other natural substances, we must use it wisely. The environment and our place in it must always be balanced. Practicing moderation keeps it beneficial and sustaining to us. And since the reverse is true, we are reminded to respect salt as we do everything else that comprises our natural world.

7. Energy for the Planet and for Us

When my flashlight needs a new battery, I buy one. When my car needs gas, I fill the tank. As I walk through my house, I see countless items that depend on an external energy source.

It is easy to take energy for granted when it is present. We may be concerned about its source, to what degree it pollutes, and how world politics affects its price. Despite all of that, we rely on it and assume its availability.

Physicists can explain what energy is. Through science we know how heat and light are used by plants, how animals consume plants, and how we use both for our purposes. And for a long time we have known ways to capture energy without using carbon-based materials; these include mechanical means such as windmills and chemical interactions such as in batteries.

I am fascinated with more recent methods to take better advantage of this knowledge — both in creating and in conserving. I'm not likely to have a living wall in my home, but I do have a living roof on my backyard shed. I wish I could generate electricity through my own steps as I walk around my house. The technology exists, though it is not yet feasible for home use.

With energy being so important, I also want to avoid wasting it. In my home I have energy-saving appliances, turn off lights, and follow other such daily practices. But moving beyond such physical actions, I am also thinking about how energy is wasted on a larger scale.

Energy is lost through needless controversy and confusion. Partisan interests that seek disunity rather than cooperation are wasteful, and any distraction from purposeful action wastes time and energy. And surely the greatest waste of all is war. One way to grasp the energy cost of war is to compare it with peace. Bahá'u'lláh, looking to a future beyond war, predicted:

> *The enormous energy dissipated and wasted on war, whether economic or political, will be consecrated to such ends as will extend the range of human inventions and technical development, to the increase of the productivity of mankind, to the extermination of disease, to the extension of scientific research, to the raising of the standard of physical health, to the sharpening and refinement of the human brain, to the exploitation of the unused and unsuspected resources of the planet, to the prolongation of human life, and to the furtherance of any other agency that can stimulate the intellectual, the moral, and spiritual life of the entire human race.[13]*

As long as I live, my body will need energy. I consume food to power my body, and I rest to conserve it. And since the physical world mirrors the nonphysical world, my spirit needs energy, too. One way to do this is offered by Norman Vincent Peale:

> *The more you lose yourself in something bigger than yourself, the more energy you will have.[14]*

Sometimes I wish my body were more like my watch, which has a battery that recharges through light. Although my body cannot regenerate through light, my spirit can. I can plug in through divine bounty as explained by 'Abdu'l-Bahá in the following passage:

> *. . all phenomena are realized through the divine bounty . . . the phenomena of the universe find realization through the one power animating and dominating all things; and all things are but manifestations of its energy and bounty.[15]*

Energy powers the objects in my life as well as my body and spirit. What else can energy do? Surely people of all faiths can cooperate to focus our energy, accomplish great deeds, and advance our global society. In fact, the more focussed energy is, the more heat it generates. If working together we concentrated on worthy outcomes, we could accomplish more than we would dare to undertake on our own. No external, physical energy source would be needed. We would fuel ourselves and each other.

8. When Someone Litters

Walking through an arboretum, I saw a youth toss a plastic water bottle into the bush. I picked it up, ran to him, and asked him to reconsider what he had done. I told him that when I see people litter I can almost hear Mother Earth crying out in pain from the assault. He stared at me, seeming to think I was a weird lady, and reluctantly put the bottle back in his daypack.

I hope that he later thinks about this brief encounter and changes his attitude toward littering. At the very least, I rescued a water bottle; at the most I may have influenced change in one person. And that's where it all begins, with one person — each person.

We know about the interdependency among all people, and we have a similar relationship with our planet. It depends on us as we depend on it; it feeds us as we feed it; it nurtures us as we nurture it. The outer physical world will become healthier when we ourselves become healthier, both physically and emotionally; and the reverse is true.

The connection between ourselves and our Creator can be found in all the major religions and many other unaffiliated bodies of thought.

The Bahá'í International Community emphasized this point in the following passage:

> . . . the grandeur and diversity of the natural world are
> purposeful reflections of the majesty and bounty of God
> . . . there follows an implicit understanding that nature
> is to be respected and protected, as a divine trust for
> which we are answerable.[16]

Given the broad recognition of our relationship and responsibility for taking care of the natural environment, what's stopping us from taking better care of our planet?

Well, I'm sure there are many reasons, but we can readily see that disunity is a major contributor. What is more wasteful and damaging than war? Can we stop financially driven overharvesting of rain forests? What can we do about politically motivated practices for waste removal and water treatment?

Another factor is materialism. Overpackaging. Accumulation of things. Rapidly passing fashion trends. So-called "supersizing" of just about everything.

Admittedly, sometimes it does seem hopeless, even depressing. The planet is in such a mess, what can I do? It's tempting to conclude that the pace of deterioration is faster than the rate of recovery. My optimism is restored through words such as these by the Universal House of Justice:

> *"Unity of thought in world undertakings", a concept for which the most idealistic aspirations at the opening of the twentieth century lacked even reference points, is also in large measure everywhere apparent in vast programmes of social and economic development, humanitarian aid and concern for protection of the environment of the planet and its oceans.*[17]

If I believe that we have a future, then I must also believe that the planet will survive and even recover from its present damaged state. I am encouraged by this idea, inspired to keep trying. I can't single-handedly save the planet, but my actions do matter. Beyond developing environmentally sound habits on my own, I can support conservation and cleanup efforts. And I can speak up in situations like I did in the arboretum. I can encourage others to do the same, having confidence in the impact we can have on each other and how this will help Planet Earth.

9. Thoughts by the Campfire

During our annual camping trip, John and I were eagerly looking forward to a roaring fire to take the chill out of the evening. Though we are both generally adept with campfires and we had a nice stack of firewood, it just didn't go well for us that evening. The fire needed more small and medium bits of dry wood for the heat to catch, to spread, and finally to build an energy of its own. I realized that a good fire requires the correct materials, skill, time, and patience.

As I re-arranged the logs and scrounged for other flammable materials, I found myself thinking about fire and its place in the world. Like other aspects of nature, it can be both constructive and destructive; entertaining as well as practical. It can be controlled within limits, and it obeys laws.

Nature creates fires through lightning, thereby igniting combustible, organic material. And then it can spread. Likewise, in building a campfire, I must create the right conditions, have the ingredients in correct proportion, and work in proper sequence. If I do it well, then contagion will take over, with even damp wood igniting from nearby pieces.

This quality of contagion is a double-edged sword. We know we can catch illness from other people. Perhaps less obviously, we can also catch a good mood, optimism, and inspiration — and the same is true for negative and, worse yet, destructive attitudes. This is what is indicated in phrases such as:

> *religious hatred and rancor is a world-consuming fire*
>
> *the fire of persecution*

fire of greed and avarice

fire of war and conflict[18]

The Bahá'í Writings frequently refer to the dual nature of fire in physical as well as metaphorical terms. I am reassured by phrases such as:

fire of divine love and understanding

lamps of justice

fire of love and affection

spiritual fire[19]

Religious writings have long used the concept of "test by fire" to indicate purification through difficult times. Fire symbolizes the means through which we build character. It challenges us to overcome our problems, and it inspires us by warming our hearts and prompting action.

I suppose fire itself is neither good nor bad. Its essential nature is to burn, just like water will make things wet. This means that labels such as "good" and "bad" are subjective, with the key factor being my own attitude toward whatever I am experiencing. Fire's impact may be evaluated in terms of its effects and my own expectations.

Heat from fire changes a substance, reducing it to its elemental parts. The same may be said for people, who may find themselves transformed through their efforts in overcoming adversity. Fire can purify a substance, removing the dross that otherwise conceals its beauty. Again, the same can happen for people, who come through problems radiant in their relief to have overcome them.

So there I was, back at the campfire, lost in thought, finally enjoying the fire's warmth and light. And dearly hoping for its protection against wolves and mosquitoes, too.

10. Green Decisions

I've been "green" since before the term was coined. The book *Diet for a Small Planet*[20] inspired me to be vegetarian in the early 1970s, and around that same time I started changing other habits, too. Back then it was much more difficult than now. Few stores sold yogurt, so I made my own. Soy-based meat substitutes weren't generally available, so I learned about combining grains, nuts, seeds, and legumes. Recycling required driving across the city to a site with bins for various colors of glass, cardboard, and metals. Difficulty aside, these were good things to do, and I did them heartily and enjoyably.

More recently though, it seems that taking steps to help the environment has become more complicated. It's difficult to learn and then apply rules and evaluate the many trade-offs. Hybrid cars, but what about the battery? Fluorescent bulbs, but what about the mercury? I buy organic produce but may have to go further to find it, often pay more, and the selection is limited. Taken to its extreme, buying local (within a 100-mile radius) would be the end of coffee, tea, bananas, citrus, and a long list of other items. And of course, such action would deny the social and economic benefits stemming from the interdependence of regions and nations through trade.

Someone asked me if they should wash cans before recycling them. That question surprised me, because it never occurred to me not to — possibly because I formed my own habits back when recycling was unusual and water was plentiful.

I realize now that habits need to be re-examined occasionally to consider new learning. In environmental terms, I need to distinguish between the goal (help the environment) and the starting point (reduce, reuse, recycle — and my own addition to this list, "refuse"). I must consider: Does it help sustain our environment? Can I maintain the action? Do the long-term benefits outweigh the costs? That is the evolving standard.

I can compare this to social situations, where I have a standard for making decisions. In religious or spiritual terms, that would be the message I follow. As a Bahá'í I ask myself, "Does this promote unity?" Other faiths have their own guidance, and their followers can decide for themselves whether they are sufficient or relevant to the times in which we live.

Another principle through which I can guide my behavior is to be mindful of the relationship between the inner and outer environment. Shoghi Effendi wrote about this in the following:

> We cannot segregate the human heart from the environment outside us and say that once one of these is reformed everything will be improved. Man is organic with the world. His inner life moulds the environment and is itself also deeply affected by it. The one acts upon the other and every abiding change in the life of man is the result of these mutual reactions.[21]

Since virtually every religious tradition has a way of stating the Golden Rule, and no faith has any teaching that contradicts it, we might adapt it to suit our relationship with our planet. We could call it our "Green Rule."

To apply it, we only need to imagine Mother Earth saying to us, "Do unto the Planet as you would have it do unto you." Together we can provide educational resources and practical tools for universal action. And then we can figure out how to make green decisions.

II. The Countryside as Home to the Spirit

Whenever I have a problem to solve or a question to answer, I like to go for a walk, preferably in natural areas rather than city streets. It's not so much that I actively work on a solution while I'm walking but rather that I find ideas just come to me. Sometimes I am almost bombarded by them. And yet, in a more urban setting, this seldom happens.

I'm not alone in this experience, and there are probably several explanations. But they all relate to the difference between "country" and "city" and how our bodies and our minds react to each of them.

According to 'Abdu'l-Bahá, Bahá'u'lláh said during one of His times of imprisonment:

> *I have not gazed on verdure for nine years. The country is the world of the soul, the city is the world of bodies.*[22]

Since we are ourselves made up of both a physical body and a nonphysical soul, the message isn't about avoidance so much as it is about balance. We might ask ourselves how much time every week do we spend on our bodies. And then the next question is how much time do we devote to our souls. We needn't deny ourselves the positive aspects of cities, but we should ensure contact with the countryside as well.

This is not an indictment of cities. I fondly remember my own years living in large cities, and those were fun and stimulating times. Urban life offers business and commerce, cultural opportunities, and wondrous signs of material progress and growth. Though now I live in a small town, I still enjoy visiting large cities, appreciating what's distinct about each and having new experiences. One part of my brain is stimulated and excited by it, and I would not want to be entirely cut off from occasional access to a city.

On the other hand, I find myself fulfilled and receptive to insights in the countryside. Free of the distractions and noises of city life, I can think. Sometimes it even seems that my brain is breathing, if such a thing were literally true.

While there, I can hear and otherwise sense a connection with nature and my own essence. Removed from the distractions of busy streets and the energy of so many other people, I am more receptive to inspiration and less eager to judge my thoughts. An idea that is too easily put aside on a busy day is finally given time for consideration. A problem that is too complex to solve when I'm surrounded by noise or activity is given a chance to percolate toward a solution. The temptation to possess things is replaced by the opportunity to acquire ideas.

With the general trend toward increased urbanization, effects are being noted. Tony Dokoupil wrote:

> *It is well established that city living — with its constant noise and lack of solitude — is linked to higher rates of insanity . . .*[23]

This doesn't mean we are all doomed, but it cautions us to leave our cities from time to time and encourage the same for the younger generations. I've read about city kids who have never seen stars — as just one of the causes of "nature deficit disorder."

Whether we live or work in cities, villages, or something in-between; wherever our daily lives take us — at the very least we can spend some time in green spaces. We can enjoy time in city parks and greenbelts. And within our own homes we can create some sense of countryside, too. Even the smallest city apartment has a window where plants can thrive, and recordings of natural sounds can be played. This is better than nothing.

The important thing is to give our spirit time to roam and to be in its own home. And our bodies will be thankful, too.

Chapter 7

Education

I. Teaching and Learning — Benefitting from Both

I recently attended a conference on the theme of "Teaching and Learning." With so many ideas being explored that day, I have been thinking since about the relationship between teaching and learning — and even whether one can occur without the other.

We've probably all heard the proverbial question about a tree that falls in the forest and whether it make a sound if no one hears it. A similar question is: Can teaching take place in the absence of learning?

Classic communications theory would say no, insisting that a message must have a receiver. Within these theoretical terms, communication requires a sender, a medium, and a receiver; and then a feedback loop can be established, whereby one impacts or influences the other.

I see this differently though, and the reason is simple. As I sit in my home office writing this, the sun is shining, and it does so for everyone, not just for me. And even though at the moment I cannot see it, I do believe it is shining. So far as feedback is concerned — well, the sun doesn't stop shining just because I don't notice it doing so.

Within the framework of religious traditions, this discussion takes on a different perspective, and the words we use would therefore be different. To offer a metaphor, teaching might be considered truths or instruction put forth by the Divine Messenger, and learning then becomes the resulting changes in people's thoughts and behavior.

As an individual, I might wonder what determines whether I receive the teaching and what I might do with it, i.e. how I might learn. The answer is that I have free will to recognize it and to act to the extent of my own capacity. In this context, capacity is more than just innate intelligence (such as measured by IQ or even EQ tests). Rather, the word refs to receptivity, lack of prejudice, and a yearning to learn and grow. Through free will I can choose to stretch to the limits of my capacity, or I can remain unfulfilled.

Bahá'ís follow the teachings of Bahá'u'lláh, and "Divine Educator" is among the many ways we refer to Him. His presence was announced and His message given, independent of who heard or responded to it. Since the essence of His message is unity, we believe that the world is moving toward unity, even as signs of disunity linger along the way.

Through the ages, other Educators have come to instruct humanity with the purpose of advancing civilization and guiding us to higher awareness. Since the fundamental truths have not changed, I agree with the basic principles found within other religious traditions. But as humanity has developed and matured, so has the message. Specifically, throughout human history teachings have been revealed about practical affairs and issues relevant to the times.

Whatever may be a person's motivation for learning, it offers many benefits. As Leonardo da Vinci said:

The noblest pleasure is the joy of understanding.[1]

So, to return to my initial question about teaching and learning, I do think that one can take place without the other. I can choose to be attentive to teaching and to learn from it; or I can choose to disregard it. In either case, the consequences are mine to consider. And whether or not I myself learn, the potential remains for others to learn and to benefit. Much like the sun shines even when I do not see it.

2. Remembering My Teachers

Sometime today — somehow, somewhere — I lost an item of great sentimental value, something I have enjoyed for many years. When I noticed it missing, I searched everywhere I could remember being today. Alas my search brought no results, other than a reminder that even material objects are not permanent.

I suppose in a way we are all searching for something. Whether the search is for information, improved health, satisfying work, friends to share adventures, or our purpose in life — we are all seekers and learners.

Seeking doesn't have to mean that something is missing or that we are discontent. To the contrary, it may mean that we're curious, engaged, energized, or challenged.

As children, we wanted to learn because we were looking for answers about the world and the people in it. And though there were limits to what we could understand or learn at any given age, we were curious.

As grown-ups we continue to search and to learn, though at some point we will again reach our limit. The reason isn't because there isn't more truth out there; rather we eventually reach the extent of our human limitations and ability to comprehend. 'Abdu'l-Bahá offers this explanation:

> . . . God is almighty, but His greatness cannot be brought within the grasp of human limitation. We cannot limit God to a boundary. Man is limited, but the world of Divinity is unlimited.[2]

As individuals and as part of humanity, we can advance through intellectual, scientific, and creative endeavors. The Universal House of Justice expressed this idea in its 1985 publication *The Promise of World*

Peace, noting that as spiritual beings our fulfillment comes from more than our accomplishments:

> *But such accomplishments alone have never satisfied the human spirit, whose mysterious nature inclines it towards transcendence, a reaching towards an invisible realm, towards the ultimate reality, that unknowable essence of essences called God.*[3]

The Bahá'í Writings present a relationship between the search for truth and the goal of unity, as our individual paths will lead us to each other. Along the way, we encounter and are guided by teachers.

Where would we be without our teachers? From our earliest days they were ever-present. I suspect we can all think of favorite teachers. For example, I remember an English teacher who valued structure and precision in language. Even if it seemed tedious at the time, what she taught has been useful throughout my life.

And then there was my French conversation professor during my university years. He used to tell stories in French that were so engaging that we students found ourselves understanding far beyond our actual level of instruction. His enthusiasm for stories taught me more than I realized at the time.

Outside of educational settings, we learn from so many other people, ranging from formally trained journalists to the person on the next treadmill at the gym. They may be concerned with information or some aspect of current events, some of which will be subjective or attitudinal.

This is where things can get tricky, because subjective ideas (opinions or attitudes) can be true for one person but not for another. Beyond that, for something to be true for someone, it is not enough to have been taught it. The beliefs of parents or teachers, blindly passed down to children, may not withstand the test of time. Rather, the basis for an authentic life is what we have gleaned from others and then examined thoroughly for ourselves. This idea also helps to explain the differences between prejudice, vain imaginings, and truth.

In today's world, where our interdependence has perhaps never been more evident, I want to translate my learning into action. If I have learned something, and if I use that as a guiding principle in my own life, then something good can come from that action. What better reward for learners and seekers than to discover a purpose for what they have found and learned.

3. Long Life Through Lifelong Learning

Visiting in my friend's home, I heard her young daughter complain about a subject that was being studied in school. In her words: "I already know about that. We studied it last year." I asked her to tell me more, since it seemed to be a subject that one could study for many years without fully mastering it. She knew some facts and figures, but the relevance and application had not been explored.

This got me thinking more about the idea of knowing. The word itself sounds static and closed. On the other hand, "learning" sounds alive and organic. The distinction between these words is comparable to what we know about plants: What isn't growing is dying.

There is also a practical side to this. In the mid–1950s Eric Hoffer wrote:

> In a time of drastic change it is the learners who survive; the "learned" find themselves fully equipped to live in a world that no longer exists.[4]

Renowned coach and motivational writer John Wooden believed that learning never stops if we are open to it and recognize the opportunities it presents. (By the way, he died just a few months before his 100th birthday!)

> It's what you learn after you know it all that counts.[5]

Both quotations are as true today as when they were expressed by their authors — maybe even more so, considering the accelerating rate of change. If we agree with these ideas then we embrace learning, and that will prevent our falling into complacency. These words beckon us to become lifelong learners, which will help us to maintain our relevance even as we better understand the times in which we live.

What are the requisites to being lifelong learners? I would put open-mindedness first on the list, because without it then the rest cannot happen. A closed mind is like a doorway slammed shut and then blocked by old information, habits, prejudices, and even superstitions. On the other hand, open-mindedness invites consultation, cooperation, and an honest search for the truth.

Another requirement is humility, by which I mean putting our egos aside so that we can learn from others, to listen more than we speak, and to be willing to say "I don't know" when that is the case. Combined with curiosity, this can be the force that drives us to investigate new ideas, consider a range of perspectives, and try new techniques for whatever we want to do.

Being receptive to change is closely linked to humility, because we may find ourselves ending up in a different position from where we started. Some of this may occur through feedback from others, or it may be the result of our own learning. It may be motivated through work requirements or an inner need-to-know.

All of this requires commitment to the process, seeing it as investing in our own growth. Without learning we grow stale, our careers and relationships stagnate, and our lives become dull with routine.

Bahá'u'lláh encouraged learning and applying it in practical ways to the real, physical world. The following is one of many such quotations:

> *Be anxiously concerned with the needs of the age ye live in, and center your deliberations on its exigencies and requirements.*[6]

Returning my thoughts to my friends' daughter, I realize that her words may have been because of her youthfulness or even awkwardness in the presence of her parents. On the other hand, I wonder about her teacher and how the subject matter is presented. Thinking back to my own school days, much of it seemed boring at the time until it was put into context. Bridging one year to the next, integrating topics across disciplines, adding narrative that shows relevance — these sorts of techniques can excite and motivate students.

Children and youth are the same as adults, driven by purpose. Education's goals should include not just knowing information but also using it. And here's another important goal: to be motivated to always be a learner. Not only can that be fun but also it can be the gateway to a satisfying future.

4. Education for the Whole Person

School started this week, bringing with it the recurring discussion about extracurricular activities and academic studies. In times of reduced financial resources and overworked teaching staff, what should be done about music, art, field trips, sports, clubs, and other such activities? Some people label them optional, while others consider them enriching and essential.

I realize this issue has at least two sides, including the claim that students and budgets are more pressured today than in the past. Trying to reconcile the differences in opinion, I am now thinking about education beyond academic preparation for exams or job training; education is for the whole person.

Through the phrase "whole person" I am referring to each of us having a mind, body and spirit. We seek to integrate them through education and community life, in addition to home and family life.

At the same time, countless cities and towns are having parallel discussions about local cultural events and venues such as museums, galleries, and concert halls. Some say that these must be self-supporting, independent of tax dollars. Yet others claim that we benefit from living in communities with access to arts and culture. This relates again to the idea of enhancing life for the whole person, beyond providing for physical infrastructure.

So it seems to me that both the school question and the community question are asking the same thing, which is where to put collective financial resources.

At any age we deserve enrichment and not just essentials. Our minds are nourished through the arts just as our muscles are strengthened through exercise. Education in its larger sense — framing how we make our way through life — has as much to do with preparing for our place in society as with the ability to do jobs and develop careers. A strong case could be made for the idea that, without exposure to culture and arts, people are less fit for jobs and careers anyway.

I recently came across a Chinese proverb that speaks to this point:

> *A single conversation with a wise man is better than ten years of study.*[7]

The "ten years of study" claim may be an exaggeration given today's context. And yet, the idea has merit as a reminder of the value of learning outside of the classroom. Experiences such as a music class, a school field trip, or a host of other situations offer a chance to balance the learning with the living.

Yes, there are practical limits, and I do understand that sometimes decisions must be made with money as the chief factor. Nevertheless, when decisions are being made about what to cut and what to keep, we should keep in mind that some cuts save money in the short-run but in the long-run cost more than they seemed to have saved. What is the dollar value of children engaging in an arts program? Or residents living in a city with rich cultural resources?

In a paper on education, the Bahá'í International Community proposed:

> *An educational approach directed towards personal growth and societal transformation . . . When words and actions are not directed by a moral force, scientific knowledge and technological know-how conduce as readily to misery as they do to prosperity and happiness . . . education must concern itself with these forces [moral values] if it is to tap the roots of motivation and produce meaningful and lasting change.*[8]

Acknowledging ourselves as spiritual as well as physical beings broadens the conversation about the purpose of education and community. Priorities change, including the willingness to allocate resources. We realize that institutions such as schools and museums exist to serve us, to help us fulfill our potential, and to motivate creativity and innovation. With principles such as these in mind, new models for decision making will evolve, too.

When I think back to my own school days, I remember as much about time spent outside of the classroom as in it. I just hope that someday, when today's students look back at their years in school, they will have memories and experiences beyond preparing for tests. If they do, they will be more likely to continue their exploration of their world and balance themselves as whole persons.

5. Falling Is Not Failing

Doesn't everyone want to do well in school and to be acknowledged for success? Surely no one starts out wanting to fail. So why do so many students fail or leave before graduation?

It remains a debatable point as to who failed: the student, the teacher, the school, the family, or society. The answers aren't entirely within the educational system, as these are intricate issues, both objectively and subjectively.

I do acknowledge the need to set criteria and measure progress. On the other hand, I am concerned about penalties associated with the label "failure," whether in school now or later when (hopefully) employed. What do we mean when we use the word "fail"?

This came to mind over the weekend in an entirely different situation. John and I went inline skating for the first time in many (maybe too many) years. I didn't find it particularly difficult to skate on a level surface or up small hills, but controlling myself while going downhill or stopping at curbs was another matter. I was wobbly, and twice I knew I was about to fall. So I aimed for a grassy slope, rolling instead of just plopping down, and was injury free.

I'm pretty good at falling, having learned as a child while preparing for a small role in a local ice skating show. During the first few days of rehearsal we learned how to fall and how to get up gracefully afterwards. Though in an actual performance I hoped I would not need to use what I had learned, the practice was reassuring and might have been one of the reasons the show went well.

So now I am thinking about learning to fall without confusing it with failing. I must be willing to do both if I want to learn or to try something new. I just wish this idea were more common in the educational as well as the business world. People talk about "nothing ventured, nothing gained" yet avoid risk for fear of failure or penalty.

John Dewey, noted educational reformer, said:

> *Failure is instructive. The person who really thinks learns quite as much from his failures as from his successes.*[9]

Do students get a chance to redo an assignment, go a second or third round on a project, or retake an exam? The very word "failure" is treated as an ending and a shameful act rather than an opportunity to try again, to practice variations, to demonstrate having learned from the failure.

The same thing happens in the working world. We read about notable companies that encourage innovation and even embrace failure. But the reason we read about them is because they are rare and therefore newsworthy, the exception rather than the rule.

The Buddha is reputed to have said:

> *The only real failure in life is not to be true to the best one knows.*[10]

Being familiar with quotations such as this, I was curious to investigate more about failure. Perhaps not surprisingly, online sources and my several books of quotations have a huge number of entries under the heading of "failure" — even more than under the heading of "success."

The Bahá'í Writings encourage learning by doing, even while recognizing differing levels of ability among people. To offer one example, I find three relevant points within this brief phrase from 'Abdu'l-Bahá:

> *. . . make ye a mighty effort, and choose for yourselves a noble goal.*[11]

First, the words "mighty effort": Work hard, strive, assert, do my personal best.

Second, the words "choose for yourselves": Take ownership, care about what I am doing, be self-motivated.

Third, the words "noble goal": Commit to something important, see its potential for myself and others, be challenged by it.

When schools recognize their role in educating the whole person — body, mind and spirit — then ideas such as succeed and fail will take on new meaning. Children will learn about accepting disappointments and become skilled in recovering from their inevitable falls. They will grow up with the confidence to take risks in the future, too. That will be advantageous to all of us, as together we benefit from what they have learned.

6. Curiosity Motivates Learning

As a writer, I'm always looking for ideas, though I seldom need to look far. Being curious has its rewards, since taking an interest in people, places and events keeps me engaged and in a continuous mode of learning.

I seem to be in lofty company, considering this quotation from Albert Einstein:

> *The important thing is to never stop questioning. Curiosity has its own reason for existing. One cannot help but be in awe when he contemplates the mysteries of eternity, of life, of the marvelous structure of reality. Never lose a holy curiosity.*[12]

The phrase "holy curiosity" caught my attention. Curiosity — holy? This is something I had to examine more closely. And not surprisingly, I found support for this idea within the Bahá'í teachings.

Perhaps foremost, we can consider the principle of independent investigation of the truth. 'Abdu'l-Bahá wrote:

> *... each must see with his own eyes, hear with his own ears and investigate the truth himself in order that he may follow the truth instead of blind acquiescence and imitation of ancestral beliefs.*[13]

This does not mean that I should reject everything that I have been told, but it does encourage me to consider the source of the ideas, to decide for myself what is true, and to take responsibility for myself.

Another related principle is to consider the timeliness of ideas. While spiritual truths are eternal, social teachings advance and progress through time. Elsewhere 'Abdu'l-Bahá wrote:

Present exigencies demand new methods of solution;
world problems are without precedent.[14]

When I consider how the world has changed over the years (not to mention centuries), it just makes sense that guidance — and this includes religious guidance — needs to be renewed and restated if it is to be relevant and applicable. As a Bahá'í I believe that God guides humanity through a succession of Divine Messengers, with Bahá'u'lláh being the most recent.

Brain research offers evidence that the trait of curiosity, especially when acted upon over a lifetime, contributes to both brain health and resistance to early-onset dementia. That suggests to me that we are hard-wired to wonder and to never stop growing. While this is still being researched, it is yet another reason to cultivate curiosity as a lifetime habit.

When considered on a large scale, we find that curiosity encourages creativity, science, innovation, and the arts. Simple examples include the engineer who devises a new technique; a chemist who discovers properties of a substance; an artist who works with new materials; and a filmmaker who tries new cameras and lights. Truly the list is endless.

On a smaller, more individualized scale, curiosity can result in new friendships, for example in meeting new neighbors. It can introduce new hobbies and outside interests, as I try something and find it enjoyable. It can offer fresh ideas, as I read a new author or listen to a different radio station. And it keeps me humble, as I witness what others are doing and appreciate it.

Curiosity also opens my mind to new interpretations and insights. I find this happens upon rereading a book or rewatching a film. Frequently a formerly overlooked detail or a clue appears to me. Realizing this is the case keeps me in a state of continuous learning. There is no such thing as being "done"; there is always more to learn and to understand.

The Bahá'í Writings make it clear that the ultimate purpose of education is to recognize realities, work toward unity, and experience fellowship with all peoples. Beyond what I can learn that is educational or entertaining, what can I use for the welfare of others? That question deserves further contemplation and is holy enough even for Einstein.

7. Teaching — Quietly

I generally resist the practice of data mining, whereby companies track my viewing and purchases (generally for their own advantage). Yet, I do admit that I don't mind so much when sites such as Amazon or Goodreads recommend books and films based on other titles they have noticed my looking at or buying. Though sometimes the recommendations are off-target, most of the time I find myself following a trail of links and exploring books and films that tempt me to buy or at least become acquainted with them.

Earlier this week, a retail website pointed me to a book called *Teaching with Your Mouth Shut*.[15] I have neither bought nor read it yet, so I am not trying to recommend it to anyone else. But I am intrigued by the title as I believe it perfectly describes one of the ways that we teach and learn values.

First of all, being silent does not mean being uncommunicative. To the contrary, we have probably all been entertained by a mime or have admired a skilled tradesperson at work. I remember being at an airport where John and I were mesmerized watching a young man wash windows. He was balletic in his movements, unaware that he was being watched. I have often thought about him and how nobly he worked, with no apparent motivation other than the desire for excellence. From watching him I learned about high standards in workmanship.

And then there is the reverse experience, wherein an individual's or a business' words far exceed their deeds. I can think of several instances when someone promised one thing and then delivered another, lesser product or service — home renovations, product features, longevity of wear, etc. Alas the lessons from these sorts of experiences are frequently distrust, cynicism, and resentment.

The same thing holds for human relationships. Positive experiences teach us trust and affection, and negative experiences teach us distrust and disaffection. And though this negativity might be reconciled through forgiveness and communications, the bitter lesson may linger.

Children learn from their parents and notice inconsistencies between words and deeds. One of the areas this especially shows up is in relationship to other people. For example, parents can tell their children to be polite and then the children observe their parents being rude or impatient.

And then there are many in-between, untested relationships, ones where people think they will behave one way and then end up behaving another way. It's not so much that the people were being deceitful; rather they just didn't know themselves.

To give a concrete example, I read about a mayor who proudly proclaimed in an interview that his town was free of prejudice and ethnic strife. On closer inspection though, the interviewer discovered that the town had an unusually homogenous population. Never having been tested, can the townspeople claim to be free of prejudice? Well, as the story unfolded, eventually some people considered "different" moved in, and this caused considerable unease. I don't know how it all worked out years later, but at least that much of the story shows how deeds can betray words.

Bahá'u'lláh warned us:

> Beware . . . lest ye walk in the ways of them whose words differ from their deeds.[16]

And 'Abdu'l-Bahá said:

> Do not be content with showing friendship in words alone, let your heart burn with loving-kindness for all who may cross your path.[17]

If we value diversity, if we sincerely believe in the nobility of all people, if we recognize the potential within everyone: Do our actions support this? Much like product claims in a brochure, beyond words in a speech and other such promises — no matter how lofty they may sound — ultimately action makes the difference.

8. Innate but Not Inevitable

I can't explain the phenomenon of synchronicity, but it does seem sometimes that an idea presents itself in multiple ways within a short period of time. This has been happening to me lately through stories in newsletters, magazines, and television programs. Specifically, they are reporting about how and when humans develop our sense of morality. I used to think that morality, as a character trait, developed concurrently with intellect and social skills. Increasingly, research is suggesting more to this than previously suspected.

While reading and watching current stories, I recall seeing a few years ago a vividly portrayed exploration into the origins of morality in an episode of the television program *60 Minutes*[18]. It showed films of real babies (some as young as 3 months) interacting with puppets, graham crackers, and cheerios. Through ingenious use of these props and some simple words, the researchers examined several abstract character traits including morality, justice, and generosity. Again and again, most of the babies favored puppets that helped other puppets. It seems that we have a sense of goodness and justice from the earliest age.

The study also showed that most babies and young children favored puppets that liked the same food they did. Interpreted as a tendency to identify with one's "people," this would have had survival value from an evolutionary standpoint. We might question now whether this is still a valuable tendency — or do we now prefer social norms that are more inclusive?

Yet another phase of this research studied slightly older children. Their behavior varied more than that of the younger ones, though usually they were generous, even forgiving. The observed differences among these older children is not surprising since they had had more opportunities to learn and develop individual behaviors and attitudes.

There was more to this study that I am sharing here, but already there is much to think about. Obviously, there will be huge variation among life experiences as well as a host of other factors including biological and biochemical conditions; physical strengths and limitations; cultural perspectives; and socioeconomic factors — just to start the list. But we cannot overlook the impact of learning on reinforcing personal qualities. A society that values specific traits will seek to instill them in children and the community-at-large.

The tendency to identify with our own people may help to strengthen family and tribal relationships. But it can also lead to prejudices and an "us vs. them" mentality. So a society that values diversity will intentionally encourage children and its residents to be inclusive, thus demonstrating freedom from prejudice.

As humans, we have animal-like instincts as well as spiritual qualities. Like animals, we seek satisfaction of our physical needs. Necessary as this is, it can potentially lead to jealousy and prejudice. As spiritual beings, we can go beyond these self-centered impulses.

If I think of my character as being developed throughout life, then I can see myself on a journey. The result will be a combination of what I encounter in life and my own free will.

In the words of Bahá'u'lláh:

> *Noble have I created thee, yet thou hast abased thyself.*
> *Rise then unto that for which thou wast created.*[19]

This passage clearly states that everyone is born in a noble state. It is also a reminder that if I lose touch with my own nobility, then within myself is the ability to return to that state through my own free will.

Human behavior is far too complex to try to explain through some selected bits of research or a few simple ideas. But the role that education in its many forms has on our character development is undeniable, as it reflects what we collectively value and practice. German lawyer and author Udo Schaefer explained it this way:

The ideal character is not a product of nature . . . Its development is the ultimate goal of all education and self-education: it is a constant challenge throughout an individual's life.[20]

In this context, education includes not only academic curricula (which might have a component of expressing social values) but also social experiences, practical lessons, and the role model offered by teachers and other adults.

Prejudices come from family, friends, community, and mass media. Whether this happens intentionally or not, we are surrounded by biases. As such, we must be vigilant about racist or prejudicial statements; and we must guard against social, educational, or political systems that seek to exclude rather than include.

I cannot deny that some people do terrible, even evil things. History as well as the daily news is full of these stories. I am not so naïve as to think that this will end, that in the future everyone will be good and kind. I also realize that sometimes loving, well-intentioned parents have children whose behavior is troublesome and inexplicable.

To offer a compromise for the ongoing "nature vs. nurture" debate: I believe that we can consciously reinforce children's *natural* tendency toward goodness, and we can *nurture* an acceptance of others. The word "educate" comes from Latin and means "to lead." We adults can set an example of welcoming others. Loving qualities are innate; maintaining them though is neither guaranteed nor inevitable.

9. Perseverance — Till the Problem Is Solved

I have a friend who is in college as a mature student. She works hard at her studies and does well, but she told me that in group projects many of her (younger) classmates give up easily. They shrug it off by saying that maybe they're just not smart enough. Or they aren't willing to work harder to achieve more, not seeing value in putting in more effort.

Some may say that these are plausible reasons for not persisting. Others may claim that this is a generational difference, that today's kids are lazy and don't have the work ethic of us adults. But to me the answer isn't so straightforward. I believe that we can be motivated, whatever our age, to do better and to persevere.

These words come from Albert Einstein:

> *It's not that I'm so smart, it's just that I stay with problems longer.*[21]

While I suspect he was not giving full credit to his own intellect, his perseverance is worth emulating. In contrast, lots of smart people lack that quality and accomplish little. And it's just as true that lots of intellectually average people make significant contributions to life and learning through their willingness to apply themselves — whether solving a problem or learning a new skill.

I often remind myself of a quotation from Bahá'u'lláh:

> *Rest assured and persevere.*[22]

It tells me to be confident in my efforts and to keep trying. Along these same lines, Shoghi Effendi offered encouragement through words such as:

The end is glorious if we only persevere.[23]

Of course there will be obstacles and troubles. Do I let that stop me? Am I determined to do whatever it takes? Am I confident? Am I happy for the challenge and grateful for the opportunity? Am I adaptable, willing to try new ways to reach my goals?

I think another element of perseverance is humility. To admit that I don't know how to do something and that I must take time to learn can be humbling, especially in a situation where I might have thought at the outset that I was ready to do it. But the point is that all of us — even Albert Einstein — need to persevere to accomplish goals without being afraid to not-know.

Since people tend to learn in different ways, for some of us that means learning through our mistakes. If I'm not willing to take a humble approach to learning and accept mistakes as useful feedback, then I will be shortchanging myself and will probably fail.

Being engaged in this entire process also requires optimism, which includes believing in the existence of a solution to the problem or a way to accomplish the goal. Einstein didn't persevere without trust in the outcome. He had better things to do. Don't we all?

Sometimes we need to be detached, by which I mean having a willingness to stop or redefine the goal. No matter how hard I try, I'm not going to be a professional ballet dancer, but I can learn to dance. I'm probably not going to be CEO of a Fortune 500 Company, but I can help a local organization find new ways to raise funds. And I'm not apt to compete in the Olympics, though I can improve my running speed and endurance. With this approach, I can always win my own one-person race.

Fortunately, not everything in life is a huge undertaking. That would be exhausting, to way the least. In contrast, making a hearty effort; to commit to problem-solving or innovating; and to succeed on my own terms: That is exhilarating — at any age.

10. Learning Through Questions

Overhearing a child asking his mother about where they were going next and why, my first reaction was admiring the mother's patience with the child's repeated and incessant questions. After several rounds of this, I realized that the boy wasn't trying to annoy his mother. To the contrary, he wanted to know *why*. That was the starting point for his learning.

As we mature and develop individual approaches to learning, we never stop wanting to know *why*. As we mature, additional questions become important to us. Bernice McCarthy has used this as a central feature in 4MAT[(tm)24], the curriculum design model she founded.

Admittedly I am oversimplifying the 4MAT approach, but in brief: It uses questions to introduce four major quadrants (aspects) of authentic learning. It claims that all learners need to have these questions resolved, and as individuals they will prefer one over the others. Over the many years I've studied and worked with 4MAT, I've noticed how well it aligns with Bahá'í principles.

The first of the four questions posed by 4MAT is WHY? Like the child wanting to know why something is happening, we adults want to know the purpose, too. As busy people, we decide what will get our time and attention. Beyond that though, there is a reflective element in asking why. The emotional connection needs to grab our attention, to motivate us to learn more. Without it, we just move on. This reminds me of Bahá'u'lláh's caution about losing time to empty or wasteful matters:

> *Such academic pursuits as begin and end in words alone have never been and will never be of any worth.*[25]

The second of the four questions is WHAT? In answering this, we study what the so-called "experts" tell us. This is supported by the Bahá'í principle of independent investigation of the truth, whereby we review the facts and analyze their implications. Rather than just accepting what we read or hear, we can consider information in light of our own sense of what's right. It is also similar to seeking agreement between science and religion, since neither alone will reveal the truth.

The third of the four questions is HOW? This is where we get practical. It's not enough to feel a connection, not enough to know some facts. We want to put what we are learning to use and not just talk about it. In the words of Bahá'u'lláh:

Let deeds, not words, be your adorning.[26]

Depending on the subject matter, practical use may not be obvious. For example, I can read about carpentry without expecting to build a house. But if I'm interested enough to read about it, then it can be used in other ways. I might be a better-informed tourist, appreciating architecture and crafts where I visit. Or I might be able to help someone else with their project.

The fourth of the four questions is WHAT IF? This is where imagination comes into play. It is the inspiration for creativity, the arts and innovation — all of which are emphasized in the Bahá'í Faith. It takes us to the future and new possibilities. To some people this is the fun part, while to others it can be mysterious and challenging.

And then, because learning is a continuous process, from "what if" the learner returns to "why" and begins anew. This links to both curiosity and a desire to grow.

I am considering how all of this relates to problems with today's educational system, ongoing needs for job training, and troubling statistics re worldwide literacy levels. We need to develop techniques and tools for reaching all learners. My intention is not to promote 4MAT above other systems, though in its fullness it can be a part of the solution. What I am suggesting is that educational challenges can be addressed by recognizing both learner diversity and commonalities, and we can use strategies that honor all learners' needs.

Bernice McCarthy claims that true learning creates change. I have always liked this thought because it links directly to the idea that what we learn we can put into action, which in turn demonstrates and inspires further change. From the little boy wanting to know why he is going somewhere to the adult who is inventing a new gizmo, through asking questions we can learn and even create answers.

II. Learning Twice: Teaching

I have been doing some volunteer work as the facilitator of a study class convened for adult learners. I was happy to agree to do this as an act of service, without expectations about what I might personally gain from it.

As it has turned out, probably no one has been learning more than me. It has been exactly as written by 19th-century French essayist Joseph Joubert:

To teach is to learn twice.[27]

My many years of work in adult education and training have proven this over and over again. The learning is not just what I could have read in a book or found on a website. Rather, it is how ideas can be interpreted, how life experiences relate to larger ideas, and how the information and facts can be integrated into action.

Within this study class I am serving as a facilitator and not a teacher per se. Nevertheless, this advice from 'Abdu'l-Bahá fits the situation well:

The teacher should not see in himself any superiority; he should speak with the utmost kindliness, lowliness and humility, for such speech exerteth influence and educateth the souls.[28]

As I see it, my role is to encourage, not teach; to create opportunities, not enforce results; to serve, not preside. Overall I find within my current experience at least three key themes: humility, respect, and detachment.

With humility being an important character trait to develop, we must be sincere about it, not just adopt false modesty. I have found that joining others in learning is an ideal situation for this. I am always enriched and humbled by the wisdom and insights of others, far beyond the mere recitation of facts.

Closely related to humility is respect for others. Obviously people differ in our capacities and abilities. And yet, we are all capable of learning, which also means that we can help others to learn. The Bahá'í Writings link learning with striving and sincerity, and this is within everyone's reach as well. As a facilitator of learning, one of my responsibilities is to find ways to include everyone. We've probably all been in situations where a few people dominate the discussions. Yet, if I respect everyone then I will seek ways to include them. This may mean, for example, scheduling periods of silent reflection, after which the more reticent participants might feel ready to speak.

Detachment, which is another requisite for personal growth, enters this situation. A phrase I've been seeing lately is "posture of learning," i.e. creating an open-minded atmosphere rather than searching for formulaic answers. This is applicable to a study situation or just about anywhere that people come together to consult. The outcome might be a problem solved, a perplexing situation being understood, hurt feelings being soothed, or plans being made. The important thing is to ensure a safe place to learn, where mistakes are allowed and innovation is encouraged.

As I prepare for each class session, these principles guide me. I find myself concentrating less on the subject matter and more on questions that the group might discuss. For every page of notes I take with me, I expect to come home with even more that I write while we are together. As I anticipate each subsequent session, I am eager to teach so that I can learn twice.

Chapter 8
Relationships

I. Pets: More Than Just Animals

One of my friends works for a company that manufactures and sells novelties items for pets. Looking through their product catalogue, I was amused by many of the items; I was also surprised at the cost of some. Though I don't mean to question how people spend their money, I do wonder if the animals are any better off wearing the clothes or playing with the toys or eating the food. Whatever may be the case, I do recognize that beneath it all is a love for the animals and regarding them as members of the family. And that is a wonderful thing.

Many passages in the Bahá'í Writings mention kindness to animals. This one from 'Abdu'l-Bahá captures the essence of them:

> . . . to blessed animals the utmost kindness must be shown, the more the better. Tenderness and loving-kindness are basic principles of God's heavenly Kingdom.[1]

Other passages emphasize that kindness to animals should be at least as great as kindness to people, maybe even more so since animals cannot speak on their own behalf. And while it is true that people get to know their pets well enough to have their own form of communication with them, this has its limitations.

I appreciate seeing children being tender and loving to animals, as the result is not only happy animals now but also children who acquire a lifelong concern for animals. And as a bonus, the children can learn from the animals. For example, there is no racial discrimination among them; dogs don't care if another dog is black, brown, white, or spotted. Their eyes are capable of detecting colors (as shades of grey), but they have no judgments or hierarchy based on that. At any age, we humans can be the same, i.e. perceiving colors without judging them. As with plants in the garden, we can welcome and even purposely seek variety for its richness, beauty, and pleasure — not as a source of either distress or dislike.

If we think about animals in general, we see that the necessity for protecting their habitat. As yet one more reason to be concerned about environmental degradation and climate change, we must give priority to the welfare of animals. They cannot defend their territory against our machinery, commercial expansion, and industrial exploitation; they cannot raise their own food or find alternative crops. They depend on us to protect their environment.

If we think about animals as pets, then we see that our homes comprise their environment. A family pet might be a horse, dog, cat, fish in a bowl, lizards in a box, birds in a cage, or any of a long list of possibilities. As members of the family, they directly receive love, attention, and a level of care beyond that of other animals.

Social animals, most notably dogs, benefit from training — much like human children benefit from education. As a result of training they can live comfortably in our homes and be respectful to neighbors. Professionally trained working animals are common, especially companion dogs. And even though they begin as working animals, they quickly bond with their owners and enjoy reciprocal love. (And I do wish we had a better word in English than "owner" for this relationship.)

We have probably all heard or read about pets that perform heroic acts to assist or even to save their owners. These thrilling stories show the strength of the mutual relationship. There was no way they could have been specifically trained for what they did, but their innate intelligence combined with love somehow inspired them.

Not everyone has a pet. Some people are allergic to animals. Or maybe they aren't home enough to be attentive to the animals. There can be financial reasons or other practical constraints. Or maybe they just aren't inclined, in which case not having a pet is an act of kindness, too. But if we do have pets, then caring for them is a responsibility as well as a privilege. They belong to the family, and the love goes both ways.

2. Family and Peace: They Go Together

John and I are home again after visiting some out-of-town family. Since several years had passed since our last visit, I had wondered if we would need a few days to warm up to each other, to catch up in some way. But this didn't turn out to be necessary. We have had similar experiences in recent years with others, when we visited them or they visited us. It didn't seem to matter who-visited-whom, because in each case we were happy to be together and quickly re-established our connection. In addition to the fact that they were delightful, gracious, fun people to be with, there was something more: the realization that we are family.

What does that mean? I suppose the simplest explanation is common roots and a shared history — biological, social, cultural. Even family members separated by time and distance can relate to this, though not everyone chooses to build on this foundation in a loving, unified way.

It is more than just having DNA in common and being on the same genealogy chart. To learn more about it, I did a search on the word "family" through the electronic version of the Bahá'í Writings and came up with 3251 matches.

Affirming the larger meaning of family, 'Abdu'l-Bahá said:

> *All men are of one family. . . let us join together to hasten forward the Divine Cause of unity, until all humanity knows itself to be one family, joined together in love.*[2]

The recognition that we are all in reality one family is both powerful and unifying. And this quotation from Bahá'u'lláh makes it clear that seeing ourselves as one human family is even a prerequisite for peace. As such, every one of us has a role in creating a peaceful world.

The well-being of mankind, its peace and security, are
unattainable unless and until its unity is firmly established.[3]

To paraphrase ideas within several passages by 'Abdu'l-Bahá[4], I can imagine comparing nations to the members of a family. Perhaps we could think of a family as a nation in miniature; if we were to enlarge the circle of the household, we would have a nation. Enlarge the circle of nations and we would have the entire world and all humanity. In this metaphor, the conditions surrounding the family surround the nation, and the condition of the nations is the condition of the world.

When I think about the diversity of the human family and its role in creating love and harmony, I find myself comparing it to music, with notes blending together. I wonder if this is what peace is: the most magnificent music imaginable created by the full blending of all people.

I admit that this is all sounding idealistic. My own family, like most others, does have its troublesome relationships. Old grudges, miscommunications, unresolved disputes, indifference — yes, it's all there. So maybe our own physical families are a parallel to the larger, human family. Imperfect yet still worthy of love, compassion, and forgiveness.

As messy as the world is today, an undercurrent is moving us toward the establishment of Universal Peace. Bahá'u'lláh promised that peace is inevitable, albeit in the future. In the meantime, what if — starting now — we all were to recognize that we are one family and our daily actions were to show this? Then surely we would be that much closer to having peace as a reality for ourselves and our family, now and in the future.

3. Children and Their Parents

Hanging out in the mall while waiting for my friend to meet me for lunch, I wandered into a greeting card store. And since reading cards can be fun, I didn't mind. My favorite one had a line from a 4-year-old girl:

> *If you'd just do what I tell you I wouldn't have to be so bossy!*[5]

This delightfully captures the essence of a child's perspective — an attempt to control her own world and the people in it and the youthful, frankly naive, assumption that her way is the right way.

Not everyone has children, but two things we all have in common are (1) we once were children and (2) we had parents. Some people remember details about their childhood, others do not. Some consider their childhood as having been happy, others not so much. Some had two parents, some didn't; or perhaps this changed a few times. Despite variations on this theme, everyone has some sort of connection to the parent-child relationship.

Beyond that biological fact, making general statements about our own experiences and memories is difficult and perhaps unnecessary. Instead, I am focusing now on a different scenario, i.e. the potential for the parent-child relationship.

At the most basic level, parents are responsible for providing both physical and psychological well-being within a loving and secure home environment. They are also responsible for ensuring the child is educated. This goes beyond academic studies, essential as these may be. Parents also have a duty to give their children a moral foundation that connects them to their spiritual nature, their creative potential, and their role in improving the world as it progresses toward peace and unity.

The Bahá'í vision of this relationship is both lofty and inspiring. Going beyond this physical life, it is the foundation for an eternal relationship, and within it are spiritual truths and lessons that are to be demonstrated through actions in this life.

Writing about children from their infancy, 'Abdu'l-Bahá advised:

> *Give them the advantage of every useful kind of knowledge. Let them share in every new and rare and wondrous craft and art. Bring them up to work and strive, and accustom them to hardship. Teach them to dedicate their lives to matters of great import, and inspire them to undertake studies that will benefit mankind.*[6]

The welfare of all children is in everyone's interest, and seeing to the benefit of future generations should guide our decisions. Applying this to a community level, the Universal House of Justice called children "the most precious treasure" and then elaborated on this point:

> *An all-embracing love of children, the manner of treating them, the quality of the attention shown them, the spirit of adult behaviour toward them . . . Love demands discipline . . . not to indulge their whims or leave them entirely to their own devices. An atmosphere needs to be maintained in which children feel that they belong to the community and share in its purpose.*[7]

Within the parent–child relationship is an element of reciprocity, i.e. children have a responsibility to their parents. The law from the Ten Commandments to "Honor thy father and mother" still holds today. This calls on us, no matter what our age, to be grateful for our parents, respect them while they are alive, and remember them when they pass on.

I appreciate seeing parents and children who enjoy being with each other. Whether they are playing or in or other informal encounters, a family experiencing love, joy, and mutual respect uplifts an observer such as me. If we remember being a child ourselves then we are even more likely to bring out the best in the children around us. And hopefully no one is even tempted to get bossy.

4. Marriage: A Home and More

This morning John left for a few days at an out-of-town conference. I am looking forward to having the house to myself, without another person to plan around. I can work without distraction, eat when I wish, and watch a movie that doesn't suit his taste. But I also know the flip-side to this, that I will be eager for his return. Whenever he goes away, I realize the truth in the saying that "a house is not a home." His presence, our togetherness, is a huge part of my concept of home. And when my own work or travel takes me away, he finds the same thing to be true.

Our home being created through the combination of the two of us is just one thing I've learned through 29 years of marriage. We share a vision of what marriage can be. An eternal relationship between spouses, it can be the source of joy and intimacy in both the physical and the spiritual worlds. Marriage creates a bond, with each partner bearing some responsibility for the well-being of the other.

'Abdu'l-Bahá states that partners in a true marriage:

> . . . *should be united both physically and spiritually, that they may ever improve the spiritual life of each other, and may enjoy everlasting unity throughout all the worlds of God.*

> *They are two helpmates, two intimate friends, who should be concerned about the welfare of each other.*[8]

In the Bahá'í Writings we can find many other ideas, such as being like two doves in a nest; and elsewhere spouses are described as being one soul. These may sound contradictory, but as metaphors for a relationship they both work. They speak to the importance within a true marriage of looking in the same direction more than looking at each other.

Even with love and unity in a marriage, little things can be annoying. People are still people, and our occasional, often petty differences will not vanish. But the important matters, the life decisions, will be determined through consultation and compromise. The integrity of the marriage is elevated through the preservation of the individuals in it.

A Bahá'í marriage is a commitment between equals, with neither partner dominating or controlling the other. Principles such as mutual respect, justice, and unity are applied. Since no roles are automatically assigned, every marriage will have its own way of managing its needs and routines. Comparing to the traditional model within North America and much of the world, a woman's role is not confined to the home nor is a man's role just within the workplace.

The Universal House of Justice in a letter to the Bahá'ís of New Zealand explained it this way:

> For example, although the mother is the first educator of the child, and the most important formative influence in his development, the father also has the responsibility of educating his children . . . Similarly, although the primary responsibility for supporting the family financially is placed upon the husband, this does not by any means imply that the place of woman is confined to the home.[9]

Bahá'u'lláh described marriage as being a "fortress for well-being"[10]. It suggests not only shared physical space (as a house) but also safety and security. Part of being safe and secure is being able to express oneself openly and honestly, without fear of retribution. This doesn't always come easily, and a marriage may require time before partners are comfortable with it.

Marriage partners don't spend all their time alone within their fortress. We leave our houses and go into the world, probably even daily.

So we can also be the source of happiness to others, for example through offering hospitality. Another important action is to speak well of our spouses, even on days when things may not be at their best. Far from being untruthful, it means keeping on eye on the larger picture and crediting our partners with being well-intentioned.

When we are busy or feeling grumpy, we might forget to offer encouragement and feedback. But communication never stops, and words of praise can go a long way. The old adage about "it's the little things that count" is still true.

As I reflect on marriage I recognize that not everyone is blessed with happy marriages or even with any marriage at all. Single or married, intentionally so or not, every day is a new experience for ourselves and the people around us. The vision that the Bahá'í Faith has for marriage offers principles that can be applied to other relationships, too.

Love, unity, commitment, truthfulness, encouragement. It may be that within marriage these take on a specific meaning. Yet every day, beyond our own homes and close relationships, we can take what we know about marriage and use it to help bring more happiness to the world.

5. Coffee with Friends

I enjoy being with friends in many different ways, and frequently it includes relaxing together over coffee. This evening I spent a delightful hour doing just that with one of my best friends — who happened to be 13 times zones away. Through technology and with our mugs of coffee, we had fun telling each other stories and catching up on our news. We both loved it so much that we are going to make it a monthly event.

I have another friend who phones me once a week. She lives 3 time zones away, and though sometimes we need to cancel for one reason or another, we both eagerly anticipate these times.

And with other friends, I connect as best I can, with email being the most common for those far away. So as much as I sometimes find today's technology and omni-present connectivity to be overwhelming, I am grateful for the ease with which we can find each other. As friends we enjoy being engaged in each other's journey, as our own life stories unfold.

I am fortunate to have such loving friends. Where would any of us be without our friends? They are the ones who believe in us, who are there for us no matter what; and we feel the same for them as we cheer them on. Statistics indicate that friendships outlast marriages. And while thinking about so many divorces makes me feel sad, the statistics do show the enduring power of friendship.

True friends are one of life's great treasures. Or, as William Shakespeare wrote:

I am wealthy in my friends.[11]

Even as I am thinking about how precious my friends are to me, I also find myself stumbling a bit over the word "friend" since it is used so imprecisely in the English language, with no way to describe the range of relationships we might have. Thus, "I have a friend who" is a familiar phrase — even though this often refers to a casual relationship, a slight acquaintance, someone who isn't a friend in the sense of a committed, intimate relationship.

Ambiguities of the word aside, I do want to be friendly to everyone. Bahá'u'lláh taught that we should regard the stranger as friend, share joy with all, and seek fellowship with the followers of all religions. As a further explanation, 'Abdu'l-Bahá wrote that one of the purposes of the Prophets of God, from the beginning of time and on into the future, is to influence human relationships:

> *With the advent of the Prophets of God, their power of creating a real union, one which is both external and of the heart, draws together malevolent peoples who have been thirsting for one another's blood, into the one shelter of the Word of God.*[12]

When I consider that one of the purposes of the Prophets through the ages is to create a "real union" — well, what can possibly be more important than to think of everyone as a friend? And once I think of them as a friend, then my actions must support this. If we all were to come together in friendship, then we would be like members of one family. And as members of one family, we would care for each other's well-being and work toward a secure, healthy, productive, and satisfying future.

When I was a child, people wrote letters to each other. And back then, school-age children often had pen pals. I still have a box filled with letters from those years, and though I seldom read them, just seeing the box from time to time brings back sweet memories.

Today's skype sessions, phone calls, and emails aren't readily put into a box. Nevertheless, I suppose that's a fair exchange for the pleasure of having coffee together, beyond the confines of time and place.

6. The Worlds We Live In

One of my best friends died to this world. And even though he (Andy) no longer is present in the physical sense, I know that my relationship with him hasn't ended. I often think of him, remember our shared laughter, wonder what might have been his insights into a situation, imagine his ongoing involvement in our joint volunteer work, recall the consulting work we had both been contracted to do, and cherish our many times together.

Hundreds of people attended the visitation and funeral a few days after Andy's death. His connections were so wide and diverse that some of us were meeting each other for the first time. He had lived in several "worlds" with people including members of his faith community, participants in his numerous volunteer activities, his and/or his wife's family both local and out-of-town, recent classmates as an adult learner, former schoolmates, professional colleagues, neighbors, social contacts, and lots of friends.

At the funeral, Andy's worlds came together. While some people knew each other already, and some were part of more than one of his worlds, we frequently greeted each other with "How did you know Andy?" In doing so we were figuring out what category (world) others were part of; and we were also opening our own selves to intersecting with others. Rather than a collision, we had a merging of worlds.

There are parallels in this physical, time- and geography-bound world. For example, while traveling our personal worlds can either be challenged, as in a collision, or expanded, as in a merging. And if we allow ourselves to be touched by new acquaintances and novel experiences then our inner and outer worlds will be enriched.

Considering the large number and diversity of people connected to Andy, I also am thinking about the "six degrees of separation" concept, which is the idea that if you choose any two people anywhere on the planet then no more than five people would be between them in acquaintance. Frankly I wouldn't be surprised if in our seemingly shrinking world the number six is more likely to be five or even four.

Surely human relationships are not limited to sharing time and space in this physical realm. Beyond this mortal life, relationships can continue to grow and have influence even after the death of one of the people. This idea is affirmed by the Bahá'í Writings. They tell us that our physical world mirrors the spiritual world, even as the two are connected. In the next world we will recognize each other, though not through physical senses.

Unfathomable as these concepts may be due to our human limitations, I find the ideas themselves encouraging as well as inspirational. At least one of the ways that the worlds intersect and impact each other is perhaps even measurable. As many people believe, and some scientists have been investigating, prayer and a devotional attitude can have a positive effect on sickness. And as in any loving relationship, reciprocity is possible — with actions and prayers in this world benefitting souls in the next.

Author Richard Bach wrote about friendships beyond this earthly life:

> *Don't be dismayed at goodbyes. A farewell is necessary*
> *before you can meet again. And meeting again, after*
> *moments or lifetimes, is certain for those who are friends.*[13]

How distant is a friend in the next world? Surely a friend in this world or the next, one whose joyful essence enriches my memory even years later, is not further away than someone who is geographically distant. And the memory does stay sweet.

So now returning to my own worlds — known or unknown, intentional or subconscious — I am thankful to be part of this world for now and hoping for more mergers than collisions.

7. Lucky for Ourselves and Others

A neighbor told me that she had recently had car trouble and used her cell phone to call for roadside assistance. While she waited, she kept her phone on, though normally she keeps it turned off. Much to her surprise, it rang — and the call was not from the garage but rather a friend-in-need. I won't add any further details except for her summation of the experience: Her friend had been lucky to have reached her.

I have been thinking ever since about this notion of luck. Was it lucky that she had had car trouble and the garage had asked her to keep the phone on? Was it lucky that the friend just happened to phone then? Perhaps it was, but what is luck anyway? And when does one person bring good luck to another person?

One thing we could consider is whether good luck is different from bad luck. In my neighbor's case, her bad luck of having car trouble turned into good luck for the friend trying to reach her. The Bahá'í Writings address this, saying that sometimes events happen not for our own good for but the good of others.

The Universal House of Justice touched on this idea in the following passage:

> . . . inasmuch as all created things are closely related together and each is influenced by the other or deriveth benefit therefrom, either directly or indirectly.[14]

Sometime we recognize events as being serendipitous, since within them we discover something better than what was sought and that could not have been anticipated. Just to offer an everyday example, this sometimes happens while shopping. I am looking for one item and find another — and it is not only perfect for me but also is now at a reduced price. Taking this to a loftier level, could it be that in working through hardship we can arrive at a better place than we could have ever sought on our own? And if so, then were we lucky that the hardship occurred in the first place?

This discussion relates to the concept of free will. I have my own path, along which I encounter a range of opportunities, obstacles, and possible decisions. This sentence from a Bahá'í prayer asks for satisfaction with what is along one's own path:

> Bestow upon me my portion, O Lord, as Thou pleasest,
> and cause me to be satisfied with whatsoever thou hast
> ordained for me.[15]

Coupling this concept of an ordained portion with free will, we exercise choices along the way. This helps us to develop capabilities and insights, which in turn empowers us and influences the outcome.

There are many ideas about what luck is and whether there even is such a thing. Some claim it is a convergence of events, while others say more than just coincidence is at play.

Over 2000 years ago in Rome, Seneca reportedly said:

> Luck is what happens when preparation meets opportunity.[16]

I realize now that having friends I can count on for help — just as they know that they can depend on me — is also good fortune. I do not pursue relationships for that purpose, but sincerity elevates these friendships to such a level that they become part of my preparedness.

Like everyone, my life has had its ups and downs, sickness and health, troubles and successes. Perhaps when I have had disappointments, someone else gained — whether I knew it or not. Life will unfold as it will. In happy times we feel fortunate. And in less happy times we can trust that we will again be able to say, "Wow, lucky me."

8. Neighbors Near and Far

John and I returned home from vacation to discover that one of our neighbors was having a party — a boisterous one at that. It was only 9pm, and since I knew them to be nice people, and this was apparently a special occasion, I wasn't too concerned. After all, it was in their backyard, and surely the karaoke would lose its novelty and they'd stop, and the lighting would not be needed after the evening became too cool for using their pool, and at some point the DJ would go home and take the loud speakers with him.

And then it was 11pm and the party got louder. As we went to bed we turned on fans for white noise and put in earplugs. The party became even louder, so around midnight we moved from our front-of-house upstairs bedroom to the back-of-house ground floor family room sofa. At 1am we carried a mattress from our guest bedroom to the basement. But none of that helped.

I'm not sure exactly what time it all ended, but sometime around 3:30am I did manage to drift off to sleep. When I woke up a few hours later I felt sleepy and grumpy. Later that day I saw them cleaning up their yard, and — yes, I admit it — I felt resentful.

I don't want to dwell further on this situation and those individuals. I doubt that it's unique. And more importantly, within this anecdote are some larger concepts about being neighbors. It seems to me that being good neighbors in the literal sense of house-to-house proximity is equivalent to being good neighbors on a larger, even planetary scale.

At the local level, we might begin by considering the Golden Rule. Applying it to the neighborhood, we want everyone to feel safe in their home and amiable with those who live nearby. We might wish for more, but this is a reasonable starting point.

My own neighborhood borders on others. At some point we join a main road, and we can show respect to others in our town by such simple acts as keeping our streets clean and obeying traffic signs. Few people would argue with this.

As we enlarge our vision, our town is near other towns. Do we consider how our local zoning laws might affect them? Do we maintain roads that coordinate with theirs? Do we keep air and water clean not only for ourselves but also for neighbors and visitors? Are we welcoming in our signage and amenities?

This idea keeps growing, as town and cities become regions and states. At a policy level, is everyone who is affected by decisions represented at the table? Do we seek quality of life and security for all?

These sorts of questions take us to the world as a whole. From environmental practices to fiscal policies, we are all neighbors. This has always been the case, but in these days of worldwide communications and travel, every day brings new insights and increased urgency.

The relationship itself calls for reciprocity and balance. I might want my neighbors to be good to me, but just as importantly I can extend my friendship and well-wishes to them. And if they harm me in some way, I need to forgive them, as I would hope they would do if I were the one who had caused the harm. This attitude, taken to a higher level, would foster tolerance and even peace.

To be good neighbors means to negotiate rather than fight; to reduce and recycle rather than pollute; to share information rather than hoard it; to trust rather than distrust. I am not so naive as to think this can be done immediately, but I do think this is the vision we need to cultivate.

Within His book of laws (*The Kitáb-i-Aqdas*)[17], Bahá'u'lláh tells us not to prefer one's self to one's neighbor; not to contend with one's neighbor; and not to anger one's neighbor. These few simple ideas, applied locally and then extended globally, would contribute to the transformation of our world. And then we'd all sleep more peacefully.

9. Citizenship – And Beyond

"I will try to do my duty to God and my country." Those words were part of the Girl Scout pledge that I recited countless times during my many years in scouting. I was reminded of them earlier today when I happened to see my old badge sash among other memorabilia. When I look at the badges now, the memories blur, though each was distinct as well as significant back when I received it.

At the time, duty as a general principle was embedded in the scouting program. In retrospect, I realize that we were being trained to grow up as responsible citizens. That is still a worthy goal, considering that I live in a part of the world where we are free to participate through social activism, to vote, and to use our intellect to evaluate issues and people for ourselves.

Comparing my scouting days to modern times, I now hear less about duty and more about rights and responsibilities. Those two words describe the reciprocal relationship of what my country owes me and what I owe it.

What does my country owe me? The list would include items such as security at home and abroad; justice; an orderly society; stable currency; freedom of expression; respect for the physical environment; a high standard of education and health; and representation in the United Nations and internationally.

The reverse, i.e. what I owe it, would include items such as financial contribution through taxation; being informed; contributing to thought and discourse through a variety of media; participating in the electoral process, especially voting; and living in accord with generally accepted standards of behavior and civic values.

These lists, incomplete as they may be, highlight rights and responsibilities of national citizenship. I also see parallels between national citizenship and other levels of organized life — including family, community, and even the world itself.

Family is the fundamental, most vital social structure for humans. It is where we begin to experience rights and responsibilities, however they may be defined and fulfilled within any specific family. The Bahá'í International Community has repeatedly emphasized not only this idea but also our collective role in protecting families:

> The protection of the family and the promotion of its well-being must become central to community processes. The family is the primary institution of society and the principal incubator of values, attitudes, beliefs and behaviors. When it is spiritually healthy, it contributes significantly to the development of happy and responsible citizens . . . Harmony and cooperation in the family, as in the world, are maintained in the balance of rights and responsibilities.[18]

In turn, the family reciprocates through its involvement in the community, which is the beginning of the concept of citizenship. It does this through being thoughtful members of the community and by supporting it in ways similar to the national level, as mentioned earlier.

Next is our relationship to the world itself, where we express our higher consciousness through action. When we recognize the oneness of humankind, our vision broadens. We can then connect our individual deeds to the betterment of society as well as our own individual growth. As explained by 'Abdu'l-Bahá:

> Man reacheth perfection through good deeds, voluntarily performed . . . voluntary sharing, the freely-chosen expending of one's substance, leadeth to society's comfort and peace.[19]

Putting this all together and taking a long-term, global perspective, I might summarize by saying that love for family will grow to a concern and respect for all people. Service to friends and neighbors will be service to humanity. Improvement in community life will stimulate improvement in living standards. We will ensure that access to systems — such as environmental, infrastructure, social, economic, legal, and political — is extended to all people, not just the wealthy and powerful. Human rights will be defended in all nations. War will be regarded as abhorrent as family violence. Abuse of the environment will be considered an assault on the planet.

Bahá'u'lláh is the first of God's Manifestations to have lived in a time when our physical planet is recognized and understood in terms of its size, its physical characteristics, and its diverse peoples. He is the first in a time of actual connectivity among all peoples, with the advent of mass communications and easy travel. And He is the first to have lived in a time with an earnest attempt toward social and political integration, as seen within the United Nations. Putting this into historical perspective gives even greater import to His many teachings and insights about this notion of our world, including these words:

The earth is but one country and mankind its citizens.[20]

After we become adults, there are no more scout badges to earn. Instead, we are motivated and inspired by envisioning a peaceful world, united in friendship. We bring it closer by aligning our individual thoughts and actions. Our reward is knowing that someday people will recognize that we are world citizens belonging to one human family. Even if we won't have a badge on a sash to prove it.

10. Customer Service: The Relationship Goes Both Ways

I've been thinking lately about customer service, having had several extremely disappointing and frustrating experiences. From airlines to office supplies to restaurants to — well, I'll skip the rest of the list. The point is that all too often *service* is lacking in many businesses.

These experiences may have literally fulfilled the dictionary definition of service, as in this one: "Employment in duties or work for another." The person showed up for work and did their duties, which apparently were to deal with the customer and move on to the next one. Put the stuff somewhere, collect the money, deal with the lineup. But is that really service?

Unfortunately, history has often aligned the word "service" with "servitude" in the sense of slavery rather than in being a goal towards which one strives. This contrasts with the Bahá'í Faith, which teaches that an action performed in the spirit of true service is a form of prayer. To serve from the heart, not because I must but because I want to, because I see nobility and worthiness in the other person and in what I am doing for them — THAT is service.

The Writings have extensive comments about service, frequently in everyday terms such as these words from 'Abdu'l-Bahá:

> Help to make them feel at home; ask if you may render
> them any service; try to make their lives a little happier.[21]

Wow! What would happen if a sales clerk thought of the store as a home where my comfort and happiness were important? What if a helpdesk person sincerely wanted to satisfy my concerns and not just scuttle off to the next caller? What if the employee cared whether I returned or not? What if an airline valued my time?

Last weekend I was at a farmers' market and waited a long time at a busy food stall. When the vendor finished with the customer in front of me, she turned her back and took a bite from a sandwich. One part of me thought, "Hey, I'm next, I've been waiting, eat on your own time." And then I decided just to relax. When she turned back to me, still chewing her food, I told her I didn't mind waiting another moment, that she probably needed the break and deserved to keep her energy for her hectic day. She gratefully smiled, and we ended up chatting about local shopping and dealing with stresses of the marketplace. I got home maybe five minutes later than I would have, and I had enjoyed the market more than usual that day.

That experience reminded me of the other side to this, when I, as a customer, can reciprocate. It may require me to be patient — to realize the other person may be having a tough day or just finished with another customer who was rude, abrupt, or just plain difficult. If I want to be of service, and the other person is trying, then there are times when I can serve the one who otherwise serves me.

II. Inspiration from Others

Many years ago, I read about a woman named Hulda who, at age 91, climbed mountains. I was so inspired by that story that I saved the magazine article in a file in my home office. From time to time I add to this file, whether the item is from a magazine, a newspaper, or a printout from a website.

Another favorite item in that file is the story of a truly amazing man who swam the English Channel unassisted, despite being a quadruple amputee due to an accident. When I first learned about him, I thought it was the equivalent of the cover story in a supermarket tabloid. But it turned out to be true.

I love going through that file folder, reminding myself about people who do such wondrous things. Children who raise money for charity; ordinary people who share all that they have; people who overcome extreme physical or other challenges; folks afflicted with adversity while keeping a cheerful outlook.

I try to relate to them as people and envision the power within them that led to their great accomplishments. My admiration for them creates a relationship as they inspire me to be my own best self, to explore and even to extend my own limits.

When I say they "inspire" me, what am I saying? What does it mean to be inspired? Literally meaning "breathed upon," the word is frequently associated with spiritual practices both outside of and within religious traditions. Applying this to the Bahá'í Faith, we find both prayer and meditation. I think of the former as being supplication for inspiration and the latter as the means for receiving it.

The most powerful sources of inspiration are the Manifestations of God. Their presence and teachings "breathed in" new guidance and renewed potential in human society. With Bahá'u'lláh as the most recent of the Manifestations, the message of unity has been breathed into the world and is gradually making its way throughout human society.

Many people find that inspiration helps them to transcend their usual abilities, prompting them to higher levels of thought and deeds. This is the case when one person inspires another, as the story of Hulda has inspired me to keep climbing. In the words of 'Abdu'l-Bahá:

What is inspiration? It is the influx of the human heart.[22]

As yet another aspect of inspiration, 'Abdu'l-Bahá included it in a list of sources of human knowledge: sense perception, reason, traditions, and inspiration. Though he also discussed the limitations of this list, cautioning that it is neither exhaustive nor prescriptive, I do find it helpful to consider its implications.

Taking each of these items separately, we can attain knowledge through what we ourselves perceive, though there are limits to where and when we are present and how we interpret what we perceive. This is where the importance of reason comes in, so that we can intelligently consider our perceptions through the lens of what historians, photographers, writers, artists, and scholars have recorded as well as through conversation with people we respect.

When I first saw this list, I was surprised to find "traditions" on it. Then I considered that word in the broader sense. Not just ritualistic practices, tradition also embraces ideas handed down through the generations. Of course, it is important to apply perception and reason to those as well, especially if traditions have become tainted with prejudice and ignorance.

And then the list concludes with inspiration. This means being open to breathing in knowledge in perhaps surprising and unpredictable ways. It also involves our being motivated by each other, to be inspired to put more effort into our own endeavors.

Since inspiration can go both ways, much like communications that are sent as well as received, to be an inspiration to others would be a worthy goal. Perhaps this is the challenge we all face: to do something that might inspire others. Whether we ever achieve such heights, and whether anyone notices or even cares, the important thing is to try — to grow and to share whatever we have and do.

Chapter 9

Travel

I. Packing and Disconnecting

Packing is always a challenge for me, one I readily embrace. I like finding ways to mix & match layers, seeing how little I can take. Deciding what shoes to take can be difficult though. And since I like hard copy books more than e-books, at least a few paperbacks will be added to my bag. We usually take gifts with us, and then as we give them away we add space for items purchased as we travel.

Before I finish packing, I have one more question: What am I going to do about email, the phone, and other such items? Am I willing to disconnect for awhile?

When and how to disconnect have become the big questions of our times. And while I'm generally eager to do so, sometimes it seems I'm the only one. Last week I sat behind two teens during an action-filled, suspenseful movie. Their phones lit up every few minutes as one or the other of them checked for messages. And then there's the gym. Last week I saw a guy lift weights for maybe a minute, fiddle with his phone for much longer, and so on as the hour passed.

The impact of our omni-connectedness has become a major news item. Through brain scans and other diagnostic tools, we are learning about the downside of it. I am alarmed by the potential erosion of social skills, forming of addictions, and even rewiring of brains. Based on what is known about being (over-) connected, both health and lifestyle question can be asked. How available do I want to be? How immediate is my need to know about my family and friends? Do I need to be informed about local news as it happens or is a daily update enough? Can I tune in to world news less often or even just catch up when I get home again?

While I can choose to temporarily remove myself from my phone or email, I am wondering about how else I am connected, aside from the technology that enables some of it. The larger concept of connectedness has its parallel in other elements of life, and these are connections I want to keep and even nurture.

On a personal level, I am connected to my family and friends. I especially cherish the role we have in each other's life stories. My cousins are a great example, as we have shared both silly and great moments ever since we were little kids.

On a larger level, I am connected to my community. My actions affect my neighbors, and my local government affects me. The degree to which I actively participate is one indicator of my commitment to it, and at the very least I can be informed about what is occurring.

On a grander scale, I am connected to all living things. My actions show my respect for the environment as well as concern for the well-being of others. How I spend my time and my resources is a reflection of my priorities. I do believe that in my own, albeit small, way I can help to strengthen bonds and influence the future.

On a nonphysical level, I am connected to my Creator. This quotation from Bahá'u'lláh (in its full context referring to the Founders of other Faiths as well as the Bahá'í Faith) helps to explain this:

> *Every one of them is the Way of God that connecteth this world with the realms above, and the Standard of His Truth unto every one in the kingdoms of earth and heaven. They are the Manifestations of God amidst men, the evidences of His Truth, and the signs of His glory.*[1]

If we think of religion as an organized, collective approach to understand and honor this connection, then we see that its intention and purpose is to promote unity, not animosity or divisiveness. 'Abdu'l-Bahá said:

> *Religion, then, is the necessary connection which emanates from the reality of things; and as the supreme Manifestations of God are aware of the mysteries of*

beings, therefore, They understand this essential connection, and by this knowledge establish the Law of God.[2]

The next time I pack, I can decide how much I want to connect or disconnect for that trip. But the one thing that always goes with me is my connection with my own higher, spiritual nature. And neither luggage space nor a recharger are required.

2. Anticipation

This morning I heard on the radio the results of a study about peoples' reactions to vacations. Research shows that the time before vacations is frequently more enjoyed than the trip itself or the feelings immediately following the return home. The reason? Anticipation. Though this is not a universal experience, reportedly it is common. The first reason given was that a vacation is often fraught with disappointments. And then feeling exhausted rather than invigorated, just to add insult to injury, people add up of the costs and worry about paying for it all.

The advice from the study included enjoying a longer time for planning in order to extend the period of anticipation. Images of the old ketchup commercials and the song "Anticipation" went reeling through my mind. And then I thought more about this news item and the accompanying commentary.

Firstly, anticipation is genuinely pleasurable. We all need a break from our daily routines and responsibilities, and a vacation can offer this. But aside from time off, what else might I look forward to? Before the vacation begins, the list of possibilities is splendidly long and full of positive outcomes.

But what about disappointment in the vacation itself? Feeling disappointment means having preconceived notions; rather than welcoming whatever occurs, we have a vision of what we think *should* be. Yet, some of my own best times have occurred when I had no specific expectations.

I love wandering in unfamiliar places and letting events unfold. This doesn't have to be an extended visit to a faraway, exotic place. One of my earliest lessons in this was as a university student preparing for a semester-long field study experience. After being driven by my professor to a small town an hour away from campus, I was told to explore and then write a paper about what I learned that day. Even now, many years later, I fondly think back to that day, including the nice person at the local cafe who bought me lunch while we chatted about the hopes and fears of young adults.

Given our busy lives and that a vacation may be long in planning and then short in duration, and recognizing the high cost (time and money) possibly associated with it, we have in advance our own ideas about how it will be. We might want it to be fun, relaxing, exciting, intellectually stimulating, or romantic. Rather than being disappointed if it turns out otherwise, we can be travelers who are open to surprise. And then, wondrous events can unfold.

Life is a journey, if not a vacation, and it is full of unknowns. Adapting to what happens is an opportunity to see life in a different way.

As 'Abdu'l-Bahá said:

> *Anyone can be happy in the state of comfort, ease, health, success, pleasure and joy; but if one be happy and contented in the time of trouble, hardship and prevailing disease, that is the proof of nobility.*[3]

If happiness and contentment are proof of nobility in such serious circumstances as trouble, hardship and disease — then surely I can consider what happens on a vacation as a good thing, too. It is a chance to embrace the unknown, to accept what-is, and to recognize that even the disappointments will make a good story later.

3. My Favorite Places

I enjoy hearing about other people's travel experiences. In doing so, I not only learn about the places they've been but also about them as storytellers, too. What gave them pleasure, the troubles they overcame, the lessons learned — all are enriching.

I'm fortunate to have traveled a fair amount myself, starting as a teenager on trip camps with my Girl Scout troop. But the planet is large, and the list of where I'd like to go is longer than the list of where I've already been. When someone asks me, "What is your favorite place?" I seldom have an answer other than to offer yet another question: "Based on what criteria?"

I may prefer one place because of its friendly people, ideal weather, great food, lively music, inspiring architecture, ease of travel, beautiful countryside, challenging hiking, favorable exchange rates, or a further array of characteristics. So I always reserve the right to change my answer from one day to the next, depending on my own mood and admittedly subjective memories.

The physical qualities of places visited are fundamental. My own preference is that they be different from where I live. And as much as I yearn for beauty, visiting places that are somber and colorless has enlarged my view of the world. In fact, some of my most cherished experiences occurred when the people were undergoing great difficulty politically or economically.

During such difficulties, I have found people to be the most gracious, generous, and hospitable. They shared everything they had, were eager to exchange stories and news, and were determined to improve their circumstances. Love of family and commitment to community shined through in hardship.

When it comes to food, I always try to follow my father's example. From the time I was a little kid he would advise, "Eat like the locals."

Fortunate to be allergy-free, I can be an omnivore when I travel. In my own home I'm vegetarian, but as a visitor I will taste almost anything. Sharing food with friends and strangers is a form of cultural exchange and helps us to bond with each other.

Music and the arts often comprise the highlights of a trip. How people express themselves is both revealing and fun to explore. All forms of cultural expression can be seen as a celebration of diversity. Our colorful human garden is vividly displayed in this way.

Some of my favorite places are on the list because of what they required of me as a visitor. When my self-reliance came into play or even the reverse, i.e. where I had to trust strangers or unfamiliar systems — those were thrilling times. They richly rewarded my curiosity, detachment, and flexibility; my sense of humor often got a good workout, too.

The Bahá'í Writings encourage travel, especially with a service component. Beyond its educational and recreational value, travel enables us to learn about others, helps us to grow spiritually, and can be compared to the journey of the spirit.

In the words of 'Abdu'l-Bahá:

> So when a man travels and passes through different regions and numerous countries with system and method, it is certainly a means of his acquiring perfection, for he will see places, scenes and countries, from which he will discover the conditions and states of other nations . . . It is the same when the human spirit passes through the conditions of existence: it will become the possessor of each degree and station. Even in the condition of the body it will surely acquire perfections.[4]

Travel in the physical world increases our appreciation and love for other people, and it reminds us to include them in our thinking and planning. If we cannot literally travel for some reason, then perhaps we can travel in other ways. We can talk to people who have traveled, make a point of meeting people from other places, watch documentaries, read books and magazines, explore museums, take virtual online tours, and find other ways to experience our world.

I'm now thinking that the next time someone asks me, "What is your favorite place?" I will reply, "I have two favorites. The last one I explored and the next one of my list."

4. How Many Languages Do We Need?

I opened the packing box for an item I had bought for a trip and found that most of the space in the box was taken up by instruction manuals. To be precise: There were 11 separate manuals, each in a different language.

Wow, so much paper, so much translation, so much energy needed because of so many languages! Considering that 11 already seemed like too many to include, I wondered how the manufacturer had decided which ones to exclude. How many languages are there in the world?

I haven't been able to find a definitive answer to this question. Along with estimates ranging in the multi-thousands is uncertainty about variations, spoken vs. written, dialects, and so forth. But does it matter how many languages there are? Even if only 11, that is too many if we do not have one that is known to everyone.

Bahá'ís recognize the value of languages as a cultural expression, and we support maintaining native languages. Yet we envision a future with a universal auxiliary language, a single language that all people learn from an early age and that can be used anywhere and everywhere.

I'm not suggesting the end of language studies; travel is more immersive, business advanced, and literature enhanced through knowing other languages. But the point is that we could potentially conduct basic communications without translation.

It's often said that English is the language of commerce, French the language of love, Arabic the language of poets. And though there are variations on this, the idea that some languages are better suited than others for specific uses is a valid point. Acknowledging the distinctions among languages is a separate issue from seeking basic communications through a single common language.

The needs of the world-at-large include diplomacy, commerce, politics, finance, security, intellectual property, trade agreements, cultural exchange, and so much more. With so many problems facing humanity today — so many ways we are divided and troubled — we would be better off if we had a common language.

Many people, not just native English speakers, claim that English is already becoming a universal language. Speaking English, I can travel through most of the world and find people who also know some English. On the other hand, I have also found that travel is more fun if I know even a few phrases of the local language. My vocabulary may be limited and my accent terrible, but people appreciate the fact that I at least tried. I also think it would be fairer if the universal language turns out to be auxiliary, in the sense that it would be an additional language for everyone to learn.

Asked about the characteristics of a future universal auxiliary language, 'Abdu'l-Bahá answered in part:

> *It must be made by a Council representing all countries, and must contain words from different languages. It will be governed by the simplest rules, and there will be no exceptions; neither will there be gender, nor extra and silent letters . . . the mother tongue will be taught, as well as the revised Universal Language.*[5]

And while we're at it, we need standardized weights and measures. This has been the case for decades, but increasingly the lack of it is troublesome. Last week at the grocery I tried to compare prices for some fruit. One brand was priced by the pound, another by the kilogram, and yet another by the quart. To compare was both impractical and awkward. I asked a store clerk for help, and she found a scale so that we could weigh the quart. Then I did some calculations to decide what to buy. Way too much work for a bunch of grapes.

Someday, when we finally have one language that everyone knows in addition to their own native language, we will befriend each other more readily. Whether through travel or other encounters, we will come together more comfortably. And then, beyond our words, we will see other signs of unity. A warm smile, an act of kindness, a helping hand — all can be offered with or without words.

5. Ideas from Fellow Travelers

Perhaps standing outside of a port-a-potty isn't the usual place to receive either advice or inspiration, but that's what happened this morning. Chatting with another traveler who was next to me in line, I swapped tips about what to see, where to stay, and places to eat. Though I didn't know this woman or her own tastes, I decided to give her advice a try. Everything went well today, so I am grateful to her for sharing ideas.

We are all travelers in this life. We arrive at different times in different places under different circumstances, and from there we pursue a multitude of paths. We intersect at some point, and perhaps we travel together for awhile or maybe not. Eventually the journey ends, or at least the journey in this world ends.

From my own perspective as a Bahá'í with a belief in the eternal soul, I might try to fathom the longer path. Though my ability to understand future worlds is as limited as that of the fetus trying to comprehend this one, I can prepare for it as best I know how. And I can recognize that I am not alone in my travels.

In the words of Scottish writer Robert Lewis Stevenson:

> *We are all travelers in the wilderness of this world, and
> the best we can find in our travels is an honest friend.*[6]

From chance encounters with a stranger to daily contact with family members, we benefit in countless ways from what our fellow travelers teach us. We read their words, watch their actions, and consult with them on important matters. We consider their welfare in our own decision making and social practices. We vote for them to represent us in civic society or organizations to which we belong. We trust them to maintain vital systems such as water, roads, and power. We work alongside them in our jobs, volunteer service, and neighborhood projects. We sit among them in restaurants, theatres, sports arenas, and airplanes. We trust them to respect other travelers, too.

These situations illustrate our interdependence. Life is complex, and we humans have developed intricate systems for coping with it. As a result, living conditions have improved, and together we educate children and care for people in need, though regrettably not yet in a perfect manner.

When someone gives me advice or shares an idea, I can decide for myself whether to trust it. I have no reason to think that a person chatting with me outside of a port-a-potty is being deceitful, but this sort of naïve trust need not extend to what I read or hear about world news. Some skepticism is suitable, as I form my own opinion as to the credibility and possible motives of the writer or speaker.

I am fortunate to live in a part of the world where I am free to investigate and evaluate matters for myself. Despite the divisiveness in partisan politics, at least we have a venue for the expression of ideas. But what if — rather than defending one's own position — those ideas could be frankly discussed and explored through a consultative process and then there were unity of action? Truth would be discovered.

As I travel though time and space in my daily tasks, I encounter other people. A friendly smile and words of encouragement can make a difference. Without having to buy a ticket to go somewhere, we are traveling together at that moment. Let's make it a good trip.

6. Living a Weatherproof Life

On a road trip exploring Vancouver Island, John and I decided to stay a few days in Tofino, a town well-known for its beauty and recreation. Eager for my first day's adventures, I was dismayed that morning when I read the weather prediction as almost two inches of rainfall. Wow, that's a lot of rain, especially for a vacationer like me who just wants to go to the beach.

I asked at the hotel reception desk, "What do people do here when it rains?" The answer, so simple, so profound: "They put on a raincoat."

So that's what we did, and we had a great time at the beach and other sites of interest. Late afternoon we changed into dry clothes and enjoyed cocoa by the fireplace. It had been a perfect day.

Of course, I recognize that a rainy day at the beach is not a huge setback, nowhere near the far greater challenges that life sometimes presents. Nevertheless, as I reflect on that day, I find lessons about coping with harsher, more trying times. How can I live a weatherproof life? How can I keep the storms of life from penetrating my inner being?

Firstly, I can see hardship as a temporary, outward condition. If I persevere, surely things will work out, even if not always in the time or manner I might have predicted. This is called "serendipity," wherein there are unexpected and even better-than-sought results. And through these words by Bahá'u'lláh I find the source of all that happens to me:

> *The source of all good is trust in God, submission unto His command, and contentment with His holy will and pleasure.*[7]

If I can be content then I can also be grateful when difficulties occur. These additional words from Bahá'u'lláh remind me to share my good fortune and to recognize troubles as character-building:

Be generous in prosperity, thankful in adversity.[8]

Mattie Stephanek, who died at age 13 leaving behind an astonishing body of work showing wisdom beyond his years, advised celebrating after getting through life's storms.

> *We all have life storms, and when we get the rough times and we recover from them, we should celebrate that we got through it. No matter how bad it may seem, there's always something beautiful that you can find.*[9]

When I am in the middle of a problem, I need to trust that there will be a solution and that goodness will flow from the adversity. Much like the tides, life has is an ebb and flow — a rhythm.

Perhaps just as importantly, I can keep a sense of humor, which is another way of saying that I can be detached. If I can accept the inevitable and move beyond my prior expectations, then I will become more flexible and resourceful. This can be an exhilarating experience as I ride the highs and the lows with confidence.

So to bring this back to where I started, whether figuring out what to do with a stormy vacation day or solving a larger problem, I have many opportunities to express higher qualities. When I find myself going an unexpected direction, I can be curious about what will happen instead.

The more I think about it, the more I realize that faith, contentment, happiness, and humor keep me balanced and enriched. And they keep me dry during rain, bringing the sunshine that follows the storm.

7. Traveling Far, Traveling Fast

Midway through a long-distance trail event, I joined four other runners for a few minutes. They had trained together and now were racing together. As we compared the difference between doing it alone (my case) and doing it as a group (their case), one of them offered an African proverb:

> *If you want to travel fast, travel alone. If you want to travel far, travel together.*[10]

That idea seems to apply not only to a day's sporting event but also to our travels through life itself. Beyond the notion of "safety in numbers" there are elements of mutual support, encouragement, and social cohesiveness. And it underscores the distinction between quantity and quality of life — or even a single event within it. Is the purpose to go through it quickly or to reach new places?

Whether we are training, traveling, or working, doing it alone has both advantages and limitations. The chief advantages are controlling one's own time and not having to adjust to other people. The limitations are needing to be self-motivated and missing the synergy from others' efforts. In brief, the difference between doing it alone or with others can be summarized as independence vs. interdependence.

We humans are social animals, not pack animals. Even though we seem to go about much of our daily living by ourselves, we are usually physically close to others. Ultimately, we are interdependent, even when we think we are acting alone. There will always be some situations wherein independent action is suitable, even preferable. Navigating between solitary and collective action requires maturity and a willingness to cooperate, even as gaining self-reliance is part of personal growth.

'Abdu'l-Bahá is said to have encouraged working in groups, as reflected in passages such as this:

> *Verily, God loveth those who are working in His path in groups, for they are a solid foundation. . . in groups, united and bound together, supporting one another.*[11]

In a letter written on its behalf, the Universal House of Justice notes that within any group we will find people with an array of aptitudes. This quotation highlights some of them:

> *. . . there are those who are outstanding because they show a capacity for understanding, for work, for efficient action, for leadership, for drawing other people together, for self-sacrificing and devoted service — for any number of qualities which enable them to respond actively to the needs of their environment and make a difference to it.*[12]

This passage is almost like a recipe, listing ingredients for a successful business, community, or project. It is a reminder that no one can do it all, but we can reach our goals through working together with unity of vision.

Traveling alone can be an immensely rewarding experience. When I've done so, I have found my own wit and resources stretched and strengthened. With no one to slow me down, no one to plan around, no one to distract me with their own needs or preferences, I've readily moved from destination to destination.

Other times, traveling with others has taken me places I may not have gone. My companions' curiosity or prior knowledge introduced me to experiences I would have otherwise missed. Sometimes we even saved each other from foolish or costly errors. And perhaps the best part was having another person who shared the day. This added richness to the travel, especially as we relived the day over supper in the evening.

My own training experience for this specific event had been long and difficult, even as I noted my own progress and determination. In contrast, the group's experience had been more lighthearted. They had cooperated on a training strategy, helped each other through injuries, and celebrated their progress. At the end of the race, our finishing times were close to each other. So it's difficult to say who won or lost the race that day.

8. My Heart Is My Compass

John and I were barely two hours into a nine-day car trip when our GPS unit broke down. We considered our options, which included more reliance on printed maps, getting advice from other travellers, stopping at internet cafes, telephoning ahead for directions, asking questions at tourist information booths, and other such ideas. As it turned out, the GPS had an overheating problem, and by the next day it worked again, though only for a few minutes. And so it went for the rest of the trip, as we had occasional use with long blackouts in-between.

Despite this inconvenience, we had an excellent trip overall. And as so often is the case, the situation got me thinking about its parallels in other realms of being. At an admittedly superficial level, our dilemma required us to use our wits; that itself is an opportunity for growth. But more importantly, since life is more about the journey than the destination, the metaphor itself invites exploration.

Now taking a deeper look at the situation, I might ask myself where I go for guidance and direction. To what extent do I plan, improvise, depend on myself, or trust others? How do I decide where to go or what to do? How do I determine and evaluate my options?

As a Bahá'í, my own moral compass — the source of guidance when I may be uncertain — is the teachings of Bahá'u'lláh. In personal situations, I can get directions by asking the question "What will promote unity?" Taking this to a social or collective level, a concern for justice can be our compass point for decision making. And then, building on that, I wonder if we — humanity — can agree on moral or spiritual principles to guide our actions, even in the political sphere. If so, then we can achieve unity of thought and action by using those principles as our moral compass.

'Abdu'l-Bahá spoke about what this would mean:

> *If the moral precepts and foundations of divine civilization become united with the material advancement of man, there is no doubt that the happiness of the human world will be attained and that from every direction the glad tidings of peace upon earth will be announced.*[13]

GPS units work or not; roadside signs are helpful, misleading or even absent; maps are up-to-date or obsolete; Internet cafes are available or not; and so on, through the range of choices. On the other hand, religious and moral principles do not overheat, never require batteries, and are unfailing.

9. Inner Space Travel

I heard a story about a taxi driver who was thought to be well traveled. His passengers, whether occasional or frequent, found him to be an enthusiastic conversationalist, eagerly asking about their own home towns or destinations and offering information and insights from his own recollections — or so they thought.

As it turned out, this man had never traveled more than a few hours' drive from the city in which he lived and worked. Or at least, his body never had. Through years of taking active interest in other people and through reading and other studies, he knew a great deal about places to which he had never been. He had a mind that integrated history, culture, architecture, the arts, politics, and ever so much more.

When he was asked whether he wanted to physically visit other places, he replied that he didn't feel the need to. For him, the visit within his mind was sufficient.

Similar stories are told about people in prisons or POW camps who rose above their circumstances and gained new skills and education. I have read about POWs who taught each other how to play musical instruments, though they didn't literally have any. They used their imaginations and simulated the playing. And then, upon release from the POW camp, many went on to perfect their skills.

Before I appear to be trying to put travel agents and airlines out of business, I want to confirm that actual physical travel is a wonderful thing. But that does not negate or override the value of being a sincere listener, seeking opportunities to learn and be enriched daily, translating ideas into reality, and nurturing a vivid imagination.

'Abdu'l-Bahá spoke about travel in words such as these:

But the spirit and mind of man travel to all countries and regions — even through the limitless space of the heavens — surround all that exists, and make discoveries in the exalted spheres and infinite distances.[14]

Elsewhere he identified imagination as one our five inner powers, the others being common faculty (the link between outward and inner powers), thought, comprehension, and memory.[15]

Considering the potential of imagination, I wonder what else I can imagine and bring into being. What if I imagined being more productive and helpful to my friends? What if members of a family imagined a happier home? What if a majority in a community imagined a cleaner environment?

I'm not proposing that we engage in magical thinking, but I am suggesting that if enough people were to share a vision then they could bring that vision closer to reality. Through unity of vision we are empowered to achieve great results. Through commitment and effort we can accomplish the practical steps. Trust in others, clear and honest communications, and patience are also required.

None of this is easy, but it can happen. If that taxi driver can travel around the world without leaving his hometown, and if POWs can learn to play the guitar, then surely we can improve our own selves, our families, our neighborhoods, and our communities. It begins with imagining what we want to experience in reality. And then we can move actively from inner space to more outward spaces.

10. Through the Window of a Plane

As I looked through the airplane window, all that I could see were white clouds. It was strangely beautiful, so completely were we surrounded. With no landmarks below and no horizon beyond the white, nothing visually connected me to the land or sea below.

Back on the ground an hour later, I wondered what else I can't see even when firmly rooted back on earth.

As a starter, I can't see other people's thoughts. I can hear their words if they speak, read them if they write, and observe their actions if I'm with them. But their inner state, their motives, their wishes and desires — all are invisible to me.

Nevertheless, people can and do influence each other, whether directly or indirectly. Recognizing this as a reciprocal relationship, I care about others and consider them in my decisions and actions. And since I am responsible for my own thoughts and deeds, I must not think or speak unkindly about others. Even in my private thoughts, I should not judge them.

As 'Abdu'l-Bahá wrote:

> Let your thoughts dwell on your own spiritual development, and close your eyes to the deficiencies of other souls.[15]

I can't see beyond the physical world of the present time. I can learn from the past, and I can try to envision the future. But only the present can be directly known and sensed. Not being able to see the future does not mean that I am wary of it. Quite the contrary, as a Bahá'í I am optimistic and believe that humanity's present difficulties — and indeed they are vast — are taking us to unimaginably better times. I can prepare myself to play my part, regardless of how minor that might be, through self-improvement, lifelong learning, honest communications, service to others, and meaningful work.

I can show gratitude for the goodness in my life by following the example of God's Messengers — an example of love, kindness, and respect to all. This is true for the followers of all Faiths.

I can keep in mind these words of 'Abdu'l-Bahá, which tells us to exercise faith in considering the future:

> *Lift up your hearts above the present and look with eyes of faith into the future!*[16]

I can't see or know directly the nature of God, but I can study the words of His Messengers. And since Bahá'u'lláh is the most recent, His Message is relevant for our times and applicable on a practical level.

On a sunny day, I can go to a hilltop or the seashore; the experience of seeing far into the distance is exhilarating. In contrast, looking through clouds or even just heavy fog, I can't see much. Yet I have faith that the world is still there, even if I can't see it.

II. Where I'd Like to Visit

Unexpectedly seeing a friend at a local coffee shop today, I invited her to sit with me for awhile. And I am so happy I did, because this gave her a chance to tell me about her recent vacation. It sounded like an excellent trip, and already she is thinking about where she might travel to next year or maybe the year after that. And then she asked me where I'd like to visit. She encouraged me to unleash my imagination, remove practical barriers, and just describe a place to her. Hmmmm.

I found myself using words that described a place and people, but neither of us could think of anywhere that literally fit the description. The reason is simple: Where I'd most like to go doesn't exist, at least not yet.

I'd like to visit a place where people are happy and healthy. They feel secure and confident. They are well-fed and rested. They are joyful, see humor in daily life, and have a sense of purpose. When there is a need to fill, people readily come together to volunteer their time and skills. Their work day is typically only six hours or so, and the work week is three or maybe four days long. This creates more time for hobbies, personal projects, recreation, entertainment, and socializing.

Recreation is both indoors and outdoors, since weather is not an inhibiting factor. Entertainment covers a wide range of arts and cultural events and is a celebration of diversity. Socializing includes all ages, a variety of music and food, and uplifting conversation.

Children look forward to going to school. They are treated with respect and know they are safe and cherished there. They learn not only from books but also from real-world experiences. There is a balance between developing their minds and their characters. And with a love for learning, they are curious and become lifelong learners.

The place itself is beautiful — both in its natural setting and in the cleanliness of the built environment. Within a short distance there is a sea (or river, pond, or lake), forests, meadows, and mountains. People usually take public transportation, though for their daily errands they also can walk or bicycle. Privately owned cars exist, commonly owned jointly with neighbors or family members. Thus, air quality is not a problem, and streets are not full of cars.

Along with excellent air quality, both clean water and power and abundant. No one worries about expensive utility bills, since everything is produced with great efficiency. Extremes of poverty and wealth have vanished, though a range of lifestyles accommodates individual tastes and financial means.

As a visitor I am welcomed by the local population. They offer hospitality, which is fun for me as I enjoy the food and customs of the diverse residents. I also can stay at hotels and inns, which are comfortable and offer affordable spa treatments.

I could go on, adding more details about my own utopian ideas. Instead, I am wondering what the real future will look like. Dare we imagine a world built on peace, beauty, and unity? Bahá'u'lláh has promised that there will be such a time — a Golden Age — though far off in the future and beyond our present imagination. Between then and now, we are progressing toward it.

In a paper about conservation and sustainable development, the Bahá'í International Community forecast some characteristics of such a future:

> *Above all, the Bahá'í world will continue to foster hope for the future. It will confidently share its conviction that, by following God's will for today, humanity will be transformed, unity and peace will be attained, and a prosperous, sustainable world civilization — the fruits of which will be enjoyed by the entire human family — will emerge and extend into the distant future.*[17]

The future may not be like I have described it, but that doesn't matter. What does matter is my living each day as though my actions help bring about the Golden Age. I can envision a world that is both peaceful and unified, even if I can't purchase a ticket to visit it on my next vacation.

Chapter 10
In Closing

1. As It Ends, So It Begins

Within a few weeks of starting this book I decided that the final essay would be reflections on the experience of writing the rest of the book. And now the long-anticipated moment has arrived.

Writing this book has been an uplifting, even exhilarating experience. I believe that sharing thoughts about daily life and how they reflect spiritual truths can contribute to a better future. And the reverse is just as true: spiritual teachings can help us in our daily life. So in my own little way perhaps I have approached what Margaret Mead had in mind when she wrote:

> A small group of thoughtful people could change the world. Indeed, it's the only thing that ever has.[1]

Everyday life readily brought me stories around which to build these essays. I never suffered from a shortage of ideas, as I found myself actively engaged, observant, and reflective. I hope to continue this as a lifelong habit.

I found that my time perceptions changed. At the beginning I even thought I could do it all in three months. Was I ever wrong! I also thought I could schedule it into my life, treating it as a day job. Again, I was wrong. While most of this book was written during "normal" hours, it wasn't unusual for me to wake after a few hours sleep and return to my office to write. When ideas percolated to the top of my brain, there was no rest until I wrote them down.

Just like the essays that begin with an everyday experience that prompted reflective thoughts — so did the writing of this book present parallels and insights to my own everyday life. During this time I have had a chance to apply many of the ideas and quotations within the book.

Even a quick look at the table of contents confirms to me that every chapter has many points that specifically resonated to me throughout the months of writing and editing.

I had to move beyond concepts such as sequence, predictability, and control. The essays weren't written in the same order in which I have them now compiled, and I wasn't sure how they would fit into chapters until midway through the writing, when I saw themes emerging. The writing itself happened in a variety of ways, with each essay having its own trajectory from idea to draft to finish. Some surprised me as they seemed to write themselves, and others went through several (even many) incarnations.

Writing, editing, and revising. How much is that like life itself? Though of course there are no do-overs in life, there are plenty of chances for do-overs in writing: It's called "editing." But as an artist-friend told me, "Eventually you have to put your brushes away." I needed that advice, because otherwise I might have been tempted to keep revising, editing, tweaking, rejigging. Rather than finishing.

I have heard of writers who never read their books after they are published, and filmmakers who never watch their own films. I do hope my own reaction will be different, though I can only speculate how it will turn out for me.

And now that I am finished, I have decided what to say when people ask me "So what are you going to do next?" I will quote Leonard Cohen, who wrote:

> The birds they sang at the break of day. "Start again" I
> heard them say.[2]

In addition to my other work as a consultant, I will continue writing essays. I also have some ideas for short stories. And I will be open to ideas and opportunities that come to me without my looking for them.

As the Bahá'í International Community wrote:

Bahá'ís understand the spiritual world to be a timeless and placeless extension of our own universe — and not some physically remote or removed place.[3]

So, for me — and hopefully for readers — the book and ideas within it will be a bridge between the practical and the spiritual world.

As I prepare to hit "save" for the last time on this essay, I see myself climbing a spiral-shaped hill, passing by my starting point as I travel upward. This visual metaphor is the inspiration for the title of this essay, as I know that as soon as I finish I will begin — something.

Endnotes

About the Bahá'í Faith

Founded over 160 years ago, the Bahá'í Faith has spread to some 235 nations and territories and is now accepted by more than five million people. The word "Bahá'í" means "follower of Bahá'u'lláh." Bahá'u'lláh, the founder of the Bahá'í Faith, asserted that He is the Messenger of God for all of humanity in this day. The cornerstone of His teachings is the establishment of the spiritual unity of humankind which will be achieved by personal transformation and the application of clearly identified spiritual principles. Bahá'ís also believe that there is but one religion, and that all the Messengers of God — among them Abraham, Zoroaster, Moses, Krishna, Buddha, Jesus, and Muhammad — have progressively revealed its nature. Together, the world's great religions are expressions of a single, unfolding divine plan. Human beings, not God's Messengers, are the source of religious divisions, prejudices, and hatreds.

The Bahá'í Faith is not a sect or denomination of another religion, nor is it a cult or a social movement. Rather, it is a globally recognized independent world religion founded on new books of scripture revealed by Bahá'u'lláh.

Note: This summary, as customarily used by Bahá'í Publishing (an imprint of the National Spiritual Assembly of the Bahá'ís of the United States), is quoted here with permission granted.

For more information, the best place to start is http://www.bahai.org

Central Figures and Institutions
Referred to Within This Book

The Báb (1819-1850)

The Báb is the Herald of the Bahá'í Faith. In the middle of the 19th century, He announced that He was the bearer of a message destined to transform humanity's spiritual life. His mission was to prepare the way for the coming of a second Messenger from God, greater than Himself, who would usher in an age of peace and justice.

Bahá'u'lláh (1817-1892)

Bahá'u'lláh—the "Glory of God"—is the Promised One foretold by the Báb and all of the Divine Messengers of the past. Bahá'u'lláh delivered a new Revelation from God to humanity. Thousands of verses, letters and books flowed from His pen. In His Writings, He outlined a framework for the development of a global civilization which takes into account both the spiritual and material dimensions of human life. For this, He endured 40 years of imprisonment, torture and exile.

'Abdu'l-Bahá (1844-1921)

In His will, Bahá'u'lláh appointed His oldest son, 'Abdu'l-Bahá, as the authorized interpreter of His teachings and Head of the Faith. Throughout the East and West, 'Abdu'l-Bahá became known as an ambassador of peace, an exemplary human being, and the leading exponent of a new Faith.

Shoghi Effendi (1897-1957)

Appointed Guardian of the Bahá'í Faith by 'Abdu'l-Bahá, His eldest grandson, Shoghi Effendi, spent 36 years systematically nurturing the development, deepening the understanding, and strengthening the unity of the Bahá'í community, as it increasingly grew to reflect the diversity of the entire human race.

The Universal House of Justice (established 1963)

The development of the Bahá'í Faith worldwide is today guided by the Universal House of Justice. In His book of laws, Bahá'u'lláh instructed the Universal House of Justice to exert a positive influence on the welfare of humankind, promote education, peace and global prosperity, and safeguard human honour and the position of religion.

From http://www.bahai.org/beliefs/bahaullah-covenant/

References

Chapter 1, Home & Garden
Getting at the Source
1. 'Abdu'l-Bahá, *The Promulgation of Universal Peace*, p. 439.
Read the Instructions
2. Martin Luther King, Jr., https://www.brainyquote.com/quotes/quotes/m/martinluth122559.html.
3. Bahá'u'lláh IN: *Bahá'í International Community, Role of Religion in Social Development*.
Memories from Items in My Home
4. Shoghi Effendi IN: *Compilations, Lights of Guidance*, p. 531.
What I Learned from My Hydrangea
5. 'Abdu'l-Bahá IN: Vafai, Shahin *The Path Toward Spirituality*, p. 11.
6. 'Abdu'l-Bahá, *Selections from the Writings of 'Abdu'l-Bahá*, p. 177.
Magnetism and Attraction
7. 'Abdu'l-Bahá, *A Traveller's Narrative*, p. 43.
8. Rumi, http://www.sacred-texts.com/isl/masnavi/msn03.htm.
Equal, Not the Same
9. Bahá'í International Community, https://www.bic.org/statements/ role-religion-promoting-advancement-women.
Home Renovation Projects
10. Bahá'í International Community, *Position Statement on Education*.
Beautiful Things That Don't Last
11. 'Abdu'l-Bahá, *The Secret of Divine Civilization*, p. 70.
Sorting Through the Clutter
12. 'Abdu'l-Bahá, *Paris Talks*, p. 147.
13. Bahá'u'lláh, *The Kitáb-i-Íqan*, p. 193.
14. Barry Crump, *The Life and Times of a Good Keen Man*, p. 180.
Spices: Longevity Through Variety
15. Hans Selye IN: *The Quotable Scientist*, p. 60.
16. 'Abdu'l-Bahá, *Paris Talks*, p. 32.
17. Ibid, p. 53.
Planning Life, Living Life
18. John Lennon, "Beautiful Boy", 1980.
19. Confucius, http://www.brainyquote.com/quotes/quotes/c/confucius141097.html.
20. Dwight D. Eisenhower, http://www.brainyquote.com/quotes/quotes/d/dwightdei149111.html.
21. Shoghi Effendi, *Dawn of a New Day*, p. 63.

Chapter 2, In the Community

Signs and Directions to a Peaceful Destination

1. 'Abdu'l-Bahá, Selections *from the Writings of 'Abdu'l-Bahá*, p. 248.
2. Bahá'u'lláh, *The Proclamation of Bahá'u'lláh*, p. 106.

The Benefits of City Parks

3. Bahá'í International Community, *Environment Development* and *Prosperity*.

The Gift of Speech

4. Bahá'u'lláh, *Tablets of Bahá'u'lláh*, p. 24.

A Walk Around the Neighborhood

5. 'Abdu'l-Bahá, *Some Answered Questions*, p. 283.

Thinking About What I Don't Know

6. T.S. Eliot, http://www.goodreads.com/quotes/115907-where-is-the-wisdom-we-have-lost-in-knowledge-where.
7. 'Abdu'l-Bahá, *Tablet to August Forel*, p. 73.

Protective Gear for Body and Soul

8. *King James Bible*, Proverbs 17:22.
9. William Sears, *God Loves Laughter*.

Gratitude for Farmers

10. 'Abdu'l-Bahá, *The Promulgation of Universal Peace*, p. 312.
11. Greenpeace, retrieved 07 December 2012: http://www.greenpeace.org/usa/en/campaigns/genetic-engineering/our-vision/small-scale-farming/.

Happy Whatever-This-Month-Is-To-You

12. Bahá'u'lláh, *Tablets of Bahá'u'lláh*, p. 22.

As We Develop, Do We Also Progress?

13. Bahá'u'lláh, *Tablets of Bahá'u'lláh*, p. 138.
14. 'Abdu'l-Bahá, *Selections from the Writings of 'Abdu'l-Bahá*, p. 286.
15. Bahá'u'lláh, *Tablets of Bahá'u'lláh*, p. 87.

Justice: It's Not *Just-Us*

16. Bahá'í International Community, *Earth Charter*.
17. 'Abdu'l-Bahá, *The Promulgation of Universal Peace*, p. 133.

With Thanks — Now and Always

18. 'Abdu'l-Bahá, *So Great an Honor,* p. 75.

Chapter 3, On the Job

Thoughts During My Morning Commute

1. Calvary Church. Ayr, Ontario. August 2010.
2. 'Abdu'l-Bahá, *Paris Talks*, p. 176.

Coffee and Kindness to All

3. 'Abdu'l-Bahá, *Selections from the Writings of 'Abdu'l-Bahá*, p. 24.

4. Ibid, p. 53.

When a Workplace Lacks Vision

5. The Universal House of Justice, *Messages 1963 to 1986*, p. 125 and 1992 Nov 26, *Second Message to World Congress*, p. 4.

Living a Two-List Life

6. H. Allen Smith, http://www.likeablequotes.com/animal/the-human-animal-differs-from-11090.html.
7. Dan Millman, http://www.brainyquote.com/quotes/authors/d/dan_millman.html.
8. 'Abdu'l-Bahá, *'Abdu'l-Bahá in London*, p. 54.

Group Work on the Job

9. John Donne, https://www.brainyquote.com/search_results.html?q=island.
10. Bahá'í International Community, 30 March 1989, *Women and Development*.

Smile or Frown: Pass It On

11. 'Abdu'l-Bahá, *Some Answered Questions*, p. 214.
12. Bahá'u'lláh, *Epistle to the Son of the Wolf*, p. 93.

Sometimes Time Flies and Sometimes It Creeps

13. Immanuel Kant IN: *The Quotable Scientist*, p. 96.
14. Shoghi Effendi, *Dawn of a New Day*, p. 135.

Needed: Better (Not Just More) Communications

15. Henry David Thoreau, http://www.quotesstar.com/quotes/h/henry-david-thoreau-told-us-172411.html.
16. Marshall McLuhan, http://www.brainyquote.com/quotes/quotes/m/marshallmc157742.html.
17. Mark Kvamme, http://credu.bookzip.co.kr/Resource/Englishbook/PDF/AG30013.pdf.
18. Shoghi Effendi, *The World Order of Bahá'u'lláh*, p. 203.

Work Without a Job

19. The Báb, *Selections from the Writings of the Báb*, p. 193.
20. 'Abdu'l-Bahá, *'Abdu'l-Bahá in London*, p. 30; *The Promulgation of Universal Peace*, p. 32; *Paris Talks*, pp. 100 and 177.

A Time for Change

21. Bob Dylan, "The Times They Are a-Changing", 1963.
22. Winston Churchill, http://thinkexist.com/quotation/there_is_nothing_wrong_with_change-if_it_is_in/179038.html.
23. Bahá'u'lláh, *The Kitáb-i-Aqdas*, p. 4.

Volunteering — Paid with More than Money

24. 'Abdu'l-Bahá, *Paris Talks*, p. 141.
25. 'Abdu'l-Bahá, *The Promulgation of Universal Peace*, p. 147.

Chapter 4, Health & Recreation
Strength and Balance from My Core
1. John E. Kolstoe, *Consultation*, p. 17.
2. Anne Morrow Lindbergh, *Gift from the Sea*, p. 38.
Energy from Happiness
3. 'Abdu'l-Bahá, *Paris Talks*, p. 33.
4. Ibid, p. 29.
Advice Along the Trail
5. Pablo Picasso, http://www.brainyquote.com/quotes/quotes/p/pablopicas104106.html.
6. Bahá'í International Community, *Two Bahá'í International Community Projects Camero*.
Beyond Training: Doing
7. Martha Graham, http://www.brainyquote.com/quotes/authors/m/martha_graham.html.
8. 'Abdu'l-Bahá, *The Promulgation of Universal Peace,* p. 9.
A Balanced Diet for Eating and Living
9. 'Abdu'l-Bahá, *Bahá'í World Vol. 4*, p. 443.
10. Shoghi Effendi IN: The Universal House of Justice, *Science and Religion*, p. 3.
11. The Universal House of Justice, *Messages 1963 to 1986,* p. 232.
Over the Hills and Around the Curves of Life
12. Bahá'í International Community, *Report Rural Poverty Alleviation Efforts, Activities for Disadvantaged Women*.
Hobbies and Amateurs — Loving Deeds
13. Marzieh Gail, *Dawn Over Mount Hira*, p. 19.
Health, Disease, and Dis-Ease
14. 'Abdu'l-Bahá, *Selections from the Writings of 'Abdu'l-Bahá*, p. 61.
Life Is a HIIT
15. Shoghi Effendi, *The Unfolding Destiny of the British Bahá'í Community*, p. 453.
Being Healthy — Outside and In
16. Yiddish proverb IN: *High Impact Quotations*, p. 155.
17. 'Abdu'l-Bahá, *Wellspring of Guidance*, p. 39.
During Times of Severe Tests
18. Winston Churchill, http://www.brainyquote.com/quotes/quotes/w/winstonchu103788.html.
19. 'Abdu'l-Bahá, *Tablets of 'Abdu'l-Bahá Vol 1*, p. 98.
20. The Universal House of Justice, *To Iranian Believers Throughout the World*.
21. 'Abdu'l-Bahá, *Paris Talks*, p. 39.

Chapter 5, Arts and Culture
Making a Bucket List
1.   *Dirty Harry*, 1971; Star *Wars*, 1999; and *Bucket List*, 2007.
2.   Bahá'u'lláh, *Tablets of Bahá'u'lláh*, p. 168.
Every Day Is a Fresh Start
3.   Ludwig Wittgenstein, http://thinkexist.com/quotation/resting_on_your_laurels_is_as_dangerous_as/261993.html.
4.   'Abdu'l-Bahá, *Selections from the Writings of 'Abdu'l-Bahá*, p. 207.
5.   'Abdu'l-Bahá, *Foundations of World Unity*, p. 46.
Superheroes Among Us
6.   Helen Keller, http://womenshistory.about.com/od/disabilities/a/qu_helen_keller.htm.
7.   Bahá'í International Community, *Earth Charter*.
8.   'Abdu'l-Bahá, *Paris Talks*, p. 113.
Prosperity: More than Wealth
9.   Catherine Ponder, *The Dynamic Laws of Prosperity*, p. vii.
10.   Gandhi, Mahatma, http://thinkexist.com/quotation/it_is_health_that_is_real_wealth _and_not_pieces/215191.html.
11.   'Abdu'l-Bahá, *Selections from the Writings of 'Abdu'l-Bahá*, p. 69.
A Change of Pace
12.   'Abdu'l-Bahá, *'Abdu'l-Bahá in London*, p. 88.
13.   'Abdu'l-Bahá, *Paris Talks*, p. 59.
Connecting with Science and Art
14.   Jeremy Denk, "My Favorite Mistake", *Newsweek*, 28 May 2012, p. 56.
15.   Leonardo da Vinci, http://www.goodreads.com/author/quotes/13560.Leonardo_da_Vinci.
16.   'Abdu'l-Bahá, *Foundations of World Unity*, p. 83.
17.   The United Nations, *The Universal Declaration of Human Rights*.
Surrounded by Beauty
18.   'Abdu'l-Bahá, *Selections from the Writings of 'Abdu'l-Bahá*, p. 291.
At a Magic Show
19.   'Abdu'l-Bahá, *'Abdu'l-Bahá in London*, p. 28.
Poverty in a Bottle
20.   *The Gods Must Be Crazy*, 1980, Ster Kinekor Pictures, Sandton, City of Johannesburg, South Africa.
21.   Bahá'í International Community, *Human Rights Extreme Poverty*.
22.   Charles Dickens, https://www.brainyquote.com/quotes/authors /c/charles_dickens.html.
The Talent Within Us All
23.   *King James Bible*, Matthew 25:14-30.
24.   'Abdu'l-Bahá, *The Promulgation of Universal Peace*, p. 96.

25. Shoghi Effendi IN: *Compilations, Lights of Guidance*, p. 37.
Living in the Present
26. *Midnight in Paris*, 2011.
27. 'Abdu'l-Bahá, *Paris Talks*, p. 122.
28. Bahá'u'lláh IN: *The Revelation of Bahá'u'lláh* Vol. 1, p. 100.

Chapter 6, Nature and Environment
Nutrients for the Future
1. Seen in Cathedral Grove Provincial Park, British Columbia, Canada. June 2012.
2. 'Abdu'l-Bahá, *Foundations of World Unity*, p. 14.
3. Bahá'í International Community, W*ho Is Writing the Future*.
Shades of Grey
4. Ansel Adams, http://www.brainyquote.com/quotes/authors /a/ansel_adams.html.
Seasons and Cycles
5. 'Abdu'l-Bahá, *Some Answered Questions*, p. 73.
6. *King James Bible*, Ecclesiastes 3:1.
7. 'Abdu'l-Bahá, *Selections from the Writings of 'Abdu'l-Bahá*, p. 252.
Better Than Gold
8. Ibid, p. 182.
9. Bahá'u'lláh, *Gleanings from the Writings of Bahá'u'lláh*, p. 214.
It's Sunny Where I Live
10. Bahá'u'lláh, *Tablets of Bahá'u'lláh*, p. 155.
Salt, Not Just for Food
11. Isak Dinesen, http://www.goodquotes.com/quote/isak-dinesen/the-cure-for-anything-is-salt-water-sw.
12. 'Abdu'l-Bahá, *'Abdu'l-Bahá in London*, pp. 19 and 48; and *Foundations of World Unity*, p. 19.
Energy for the Planet and for Us
13. Bahá'u'lláh, *The Proclamation of Bahá'u'lláh*, p. xii.
14. Norman Vincent Peale, http://www.brainyquote.com/quotes/ quotes/n/normanvinc386105.html .
15. 'Abdu'l-Bahá, *Foundations of World Unity*, p. 58.
When Someone Litters
16. Bahá'í International Community, Oct 1987, *The Bahá'í Statement on Nature*.
17. The Universal House of Justice (Commissioned by -), *Century of Light*, p. 128.
Thoughts by the Campfire
18. 'Abdu'l-Bahá, *A Traveller's Narrative,* pp. 42, 76, 56 and 62.

19. 'Abdu'l-Bahá, *Paris Talks, p. 25;* 'Abdu'l-Bahá, *A Traveller's Narrative,* p. 76; Bahá'u'lláh, *Tablets of Bahá'u'lláh*, p. 74; and 'Abdu'l-Bahá, *'Abdu'l-Bahá in London*, p. 94.

Green Decisions
20. Frances Moore Lappe, *Diet for a Small Planet.*
21. Shoghi Effendi, *Compilations, The Compilation of Compilations Vol. I*, p. 84.

The Countryside as Home to the Spirit
22. Bahá'u'lláh IN: *The Revelation of Bahá'u'lláh Vol. 3*, p. 416.
23. Tony Dokoupil, "Zombie Apocalypse", *Newsweek* 16 June 2012, p. 7.

Chapter 7, Education
Teaching and Learning — Benefitting from Both
1. Leonardo da Vinci, http://www.brainyquote.com/quotes/quotes /l/leonardoda154285.html.

Remembering My Teachers
2. 'Abdu'l-Bahá, *The Promulgation of Universal Peace*, p. 274.
3. The Universal House of Justice, *The Promise of World Peace*, p. 1.

Long Life Through Lifelong Learning
4. Eric Hoffer, http://www.goodreads.com/quotes/146081-in-a-time-of-drastic-change-it-is-the-learners.
5. John Wooden, http://www.espn.com/mens-college-basketball/news/story?id=5249709.
6. Bahá'u'lláh, *The Proclamation of Bahá'u'lláh*, p. 116.

Education for the Whole Person
7. Chinese proverb http://www.searchquotes.com/quotation/ A_single_conversation_with_a_wise_man_is_better_than_ten_years_of _study./3342/.
8. Bahá'í International Community, *Position Statement on Education.*

Falling Is Not Failing
9. John Dewey, http://www.brainyquote.com/quotes/quotes/j/ johndewey121337.html.
10. The Buddha, http://www.brainyquote.com/quotes/quotes/b /buddha118090.html.
11. 'Abdu'l-Bahá, *Selections from the Writings of 'Abdu'l-Bahá*, p. 35.

Curiosity Motivates Learning
12. Albert Einstein, http://www.quotationspage.com/quote/9316.html.
13. 'Abdu'l-Bahá, *The Promulgation of Universal Peace*, p. 454.
14. 'Abdu'l-Bahá, *Foundations of World Unity*, p. 83.

Teaching — Quietly
15. Donald Finkel, *Teaching with Your Mouth Shut.*

16. Bahá'u'lláh, *Gleanings from the Writings of Bahá'u'lláh*, p. 305.
17. 'Abdu'l-Bahá, *Paris Talks*, p. 16.

Innate but Not Inevitable

18. Lesley Stahl, "The Baby Lab", 2012.
https://www.youtube.com/watch?v=aIc-4h9RIvY.
19. Bahá'u'lláh, *The Arabic Hidden Words*, p. 10.
20. Udo Schaefer, *Bahá'í Ethics in Light of Scripture*, Vol. 2, p. 26.

Perseverance — Till the Problem Is Solved

21. Albert Einstein, http://www.brainyquote.com/quotes/quotes/a/
alberteins106192.html.
22. Bahá'u'lláh, *The Summons of the Lord of Hosts*, p. 156.
23. Shoghi Effendi, *Arohanui - Letters to New Zealand*, p. 22.

Learning Through Questions

24. Bernice McCarthy and 4MAT(tm), http://aboutlearning.com/.
25. Bahá'u'lláh, *Tablets of Bahá'u'lláh*, p. 169.
26. Bahá'u'lláh, *The Persian Hidden Words*, p. 37.

Learning Twice: Teaching

27. Joseph Joubert, http://thinkexist.com/quotation/to_teach_is_to_
learn_twice/7984.html.
28. 'Abdu'l-Bahá, *Selections from the Writings of 'Abdu'l-Bahá*, p. 30.

Chapter 8, Relationships

Pets: More Than Just Animals

1. 'Abdu'l-Bahá, *Selections from the Writings of 'Abdu'l-Bahá*, p. 159.

Family and Peace: They Go Together

2. 'Abdu'l-Bahá, *Paris Talks*, pp. 138 and 123.
3. Bahá'u'lláh, *Gleanings from the Writings of Bahá'u'lláh*, p. 286.
4. 'Abdu'l-Bahá, *Foundations of World Unity*, p. 100.

Children and Their Parents

5. Leanin' Tree, Boulder, Colorado, USA.
6. 'Abdu'l-Bahá, *Selections from the Writings of 'Abdu'l-Bahá*, p. 129.
7. The Universal House of Justice, *Ridvan 157*, 2000, p. 8.

Marriage: A Home and More

8. 'Abdu'l-Bahá, *Selections from the Writings of 'Abdu'l-Bahá*, pp. 118 and 122.
9. The Universal House of Justice, *Messages 1963 to 1986*, p. 472.
10. Bahá'u'lláh, *The Kitáb-i-Aqdas*, p. 205.

Coffee with Friends

11. William Shakespeare, http://allpoetry.com/quote/by/
William_Shakespeare.
12. 'Abdu'l-Bahá, *The Secret of Divine Civilization*, p. 73.

The Worlds We Live In

13. Richard Bach, *Illusions: The Adventures of a Reluctant Messiah*, p. 174.

Lucky for Ourselves and Others

14. The Universal House of Justice, *Gaia Concept, Nature*, p. 1.

15. The Báb, *Compilations, Bahá'í Prayers*, p. 55.

16. Seneca http://www.quotationspage.com/quote/4576.html.

Neighbors Near and Far

17. Bahá'u'lláh, *The Kitáb-i-Aqdas*, p. 161.

Citizenship — And Beyond

18. Bahá'í International Community, *Sustainable Communities in an Integrating World* and *Family in a World Community*.

19. 'Abdu'l-Bahá, *Selections from the Writings of 'Abdu'l-Bahá*, p. 115.

20. Bahá'u'lláh, *The Proclamation of Bahá'u'lláh*, p. 116.

Customer Service: The Relationship Goes Both Ways

21. 'Abdu'l-Bahá, *Paris Talks*, p. 15.

Inspiration from Others

22. 'Abdu'l-Bahá, *Foundations of World Unity*, p. 46.

Chapter 9, Travel

Packing and Disconnecting

1. Bahá'u'lláh, *Gleanings from the Writings of Bahá'u'lláh*, p. 50.

2. 'Abdu'l-Bahá, *Some Answered Questions*, p. 158.

Anticipation

3. 'Abdu'l-Bahá IN: Esselmont, *Bahá'u'lláh and the New Era*, p. 67.

My Favorite Places

4. 'Abdu'l-Bahá, *Some Answered Questions*, p. 200.

How Many Languages Do We Need?

5. 'Abdu'l-Bahá, *'Abdu'l-Bahá in London*, p. 94.

Ideas from Fellow Travelers

6. Robert Lewis Stevenson, http://www.brainyquote.com/quotes/authors/r/robert_louis_stevenson.html.

Living a Waterproof Life

7. Bahá'u'lláh, *Tablets of Bahá'u'lláh*, p. 153.

8. Bahá'u'lláh, *Epistle to the Son of the Wolf*, p. 93.

9. Mattie Stephanek, http://www.brainyquote.com/quotes/quotes/m/mattiestep543005.html.

Traveling Far, Traveling Fast

10. African proverb http://www.kmafrica.com/group.communications. poster.travel.alone.travel.together.

11. 'Abdu'l-Bahá IN: Stockman, *The Bahá'í Faith: A Guide for the Perplexed*, p. 11.

12. The Universal House of Justice, *written on behalf of the Universal House of Justice to a National Spiritual Assembly.*

My Heart Is My Compass
13. 'Abdu'l-Bahá, *The Promulgation of Universal Peace*, p. 109.

Inner Space Travel
14. 'Abdu'l-Bahá, *Some Answered Questions*, p. 241.

Through the Window of a Plane
15. 'Abdu'l-Bahá, *Selections from the Writings of 'Abdu'l-Bahá*, p. 203.
16. 'Abdu'l-Bahá, *Paris Talks*, p. 69.

Where I'd Like to Visit
17. The Bahá'í International Community, *Conservation and Sustainable Development in the Bahá'í Faith.*

Chapter 10, In Closing
As It Ends, So It Begins
1. Margaret Mead, http://www.quotationspage.com/quote/33522.html.
2. Leonard Cohen, "Anthem".
3. Bahá'í International Community, *The Bahá'í Magazine.*

Works Cited

Works of the Báb

Selections from the Writings of the Báb. Compiled by the Research Department of the Universal House of Justice. Translated by Habib Taherzadeh et al. Haifa: Bahá'í World Centre. 1976.

Works of Bahá'u'lláh

Epistle to the Son of the Wolf, Translated by Shoghi Effendi. 1st pocket-size ed. Wilmette, IL: Bahá'í Publishing Trust. 1988.

Gleanings from the Writings of Bahá'u'lláh. Translated by Shoghi Effendi. Wilmette, IL: Bahá'í Publishing. 2005.

Tablets of Bahá'u'lláh revealed after the Kitábi-i-Aqdas. Compiled by the Research Department of the Universal House of Justice. Translated by Habib Taherzadeh et al. Wilmette, IL: 1988.

The Arabic Hidden Words. Translated by Shoghi Effendi. London: Nightingale Books, an imprint of The Bahá'í Publishing Trust. 1992.

The Kitáb-i-Aqdas: The Most Holy Book. 1st pocket-sized ed. Wilmette, IL: Bahá'í Publishing Trust. 1993.

The Kitáb-i-Íqan: The Book of Certitude. Translated by Shoghi Effendi. Wilmette, IL: Bahá'í Publishing. 2003.

The Persian Hidden Words. Translated by Shoghi Effendi. London: Nightingale Books, an imprint of The Bahá'í Publishing Trust. 1992.

The Proclamation of Bahá'u'lláh. Haifa, Israel: Bahá'í World Center. 1967.

The Summons of the Lord of Hosts. Wilmette, IL: Bahá'í Publishing. 2006.

Works of 'Abdu'l-Bahá

A Traveller's Narrative. Wilmette, IL: Bahá'í Publishing Trust. 1980.

'Abdu'l-Bahá in London: Addresses and Notes of Conversations. London: Bahá'í Publishing Trust. 1982.

Foundations of World Unity. Wilmette, IL: Bahá'í Publishing Trust. 1979.

Paris Talks: Addresses Given by 'Abdu'l-Bahá in Paris in 1911. Wilmette, IL: Bahá'í Publishing. 2006.

Selections from the Writings of 'Abdu'l-Bahá. Compiled by the Research Department of the Universal House of Justice. Translated by a Committee at the Bahá'í World Center and by Marzieh Gail. 1st pocket-sized ed. Wilmette, IL: Bahá'í Publishing Trust. 1996.

So Great an Honor. The National Spiritual Assembly of the United States. Wilmette, IL: Bahá'í Publishing Trust. 2000.

Some Answered Questions. Compiled and translated by Laura Clifford Barney. Wilmette, IL: Bahá'í Publishing Trust. 2008.

Tablet to August Forel. IN: *The Bahá'í World, Vol. 15, Haifa, Israel.* 1973.

Tablets of 'Abdu'l-Bahá. Wilmette, IL: US Bahá'í Publishing Trust. 1930.

The Promulgation of Universal Peace: Talks Delivered by 'Abdu'l-Bahá during His Visit to the United States and Canada in 1912. Compiled by Howard MacNutt. New ed. Wilmette, IL: Bahá'í Publishing. 2007.

The Secret of Divine Civilization. Wilmette, IL: US Bahá'í Publishing Trust. 1990.

Works of Shoghi Effendi

Arohanui - Letters to New Zealand. Bahá'í Publishing Trust of Suva, Fiji Islands. 1982.

Dawn of a New Day. New Delhi, India: Bahá'í Publishing Trust. 1923.

Letter written on behalf of Shoghi Effendi to the Bahá'í Inter-Racial Committee of the National Spiritual Assembly of the United States, 27 May 1957.

Letter written on behalf of the Guardian to an individual believer. August 1932: Bahá'í News, No. 68, p. 3, 11, 32.

The Unfolding Destiny of the British Bahá'í Community. UK Publishing Trust. 1981.

The World Order of Bahá'u'lláh. Wilmette, IL: Bahá'í Publishing Trust. 1974.

Works of The Universal House of Justice

Century of Light. Commissioned by The Universal House of Justice. 2001.

Gaia Concept, Nature. 08 June 1992.

Messages 1963 to 1986.

Ridvan 157. 2000.

Science and Religion. 13 August 1997.

Second Message to World Congress. 26 November 1992.

The Bahá'í World, Vol 4. Haifa, Israel: Bahá'í World Centre. 1930-1932.

The Bahá'í World, Vol 15. Haifa, Israel: Bahá'í World Centre. 1968-1973.

The Promise of World Peace. October 1985.

To Iranian Believers Throughout the World, BAHA 154 (translated from Persian). March 1997.

Written on behalf of the Universal House of Justice to a National Spiritual Assembly. 06 November 1994.

Works of the Bahá'í International Community

Conservation and Sustainable Development in the Bahá'í Faith. 06 April 1995.

Earth Charter 1992. 06 June 1992.

Environment Development. 06 August 1990.

Family in a World Community. 25 November 1993.

Human Rights Extreme Poverty. 17 August 1994.

Position Statement on Education. 02 January 1989.

Prosperity. 06 March 1995.

Report Rural Poverty Alleviation Efforts, Activities for Disadvantaged Women. 16 November 1991.

Role of Religion in Social Development. 24 August 1994.

Sustainable Communities in an Integrating World. 30 May 1996.

The Bahá'í Magazine. 1992.

The Bahá'í Statement on Nature. 1987.

Two Bahá'í International Community Projects Camero. 30 April 1996.

Wellspring of Guidance, Messages of the Universal House of Justice: 1963-1968.

Who Is Writing the Future. February 1999.

Women and Development. 30 March 1989.

Bahá'í Compilations

Bahá'í Prayers: A Selection of Prayers Revealed by Bahá'u'lláh, the Báb, and 'Abdu'l-Bahá. New Ed. Wilmette, IL: Bahá'í Publishing Trust. 2002.

Developing Distinctive Bahá'í Communities: Guidelines for Spiritual Assemblies. Wilmette, IL: National Spiritual Assembly of the Bahá'ís of the United States. 1998.

The Compilation of Compilations, Vol. 1. Mona Vale, Australia: Bahá'í Publications Australia. 1991.

Unlocking the Power of Action. Prepared by the Research Department of the Universal House of Justice. Haifa, Israel: Bahá'í World Centre. 2008.

Other Works

Bach, Richard. *Illusions: The Adventures of a Reluctant Messiah*. Dell Publishing Co., Inc. New York, NY. 1977.

Crump, Barry. *The Life and Times of a Good Keen Man*. Barry Crump Associates. Opotiki, New Zealand. 1992.

Esselmont, John. *Bahá'u'lláh and the New Era*. Wilmette, IL: Bahá'í Publishing. 1980.

Finkel, Donald. *Teaching with Your Mouth Shut*. Portsmouth, NH: Heinemann Educational Book. 2000.

Gail, Marzieh. *Dawn Over Mount Hira*. Herts, UK: George Ronald. 1976.

Hornby, Helen. comp. *Lights of Guidance*. New Ed. New Delhi: Bahá'í Publishing Trust. 1999.

Horvitz, Leslie Alan. *The Quotable Scientist*. New York: McGraw-Hill. 2000.

King James Version, The Holy Bible, Cambridge Edition: 1769.

Kolstoe, John E. *Consultation: A Universal Lamp of Guidance*. Herts, UK: George Ronald. 1988.

Lappe, Frances Moore. *Diet for a Small Planet*. Ballantine Books, New York, NY. 1971.

Lindbergh, Anne Morrow. *Gift from the Sea*, Pantheon Books, New York, NY. 2005 (Reprint).

Newsweek Magazine. Newsweek Inc., New York, NY.

Ponder, Catherine. *The Dynamic Laws of Prosperity*. Englewood Cliffs, NJ: Prentice-Hall, Inc. 1962.

Pound, Richard W. comp. *High Impact Quotations*. Markham, Ontario, Canada: Fitzhenry & Whiteside. 2004.

Schaefer, Udo. *Bahá'í Ethics in Light of Scripture*, *Vol. 2*. Herts, UK: George Ronald. 2007.

Sears, William. *God Loves Laughter*. Herts, UK: George Ronald. 1968.

Selye, Hans. *The Quotable Scientist*. New York: McGraw-Hill. 2000.

Stockman, Robert. *The Bahá'í Faith: A Guide for the Perplexed*. London, England: Bloomsbury Academic. 2012.

Taherzadeh, Adib. *The Revelation of Bahá'u'lláh Vol. 1*. Herts, UK: George Ronald. 1974.

Taherzadeh, Adib. *The Revelation of Baha'u'llah Vol. 3*. Herts, UK: George Ronald. 1974.

UN General Assembly. *Universal Declaration of Human Rights*. 10 December 1948.

Vafai, Shahin. *The Path Toward Spirituality*. West Palm Beach, FL: Palabra Publications. 1998.

Recorded Media

Anthem. Leonard Cohen. Waiting for the Miracle. Columbia Label, New York City, 1992. Studio Album.

Beautiful Boy. John Lennon. Double Fantasy, The Hit Factory, New York City, 1980. Studio Album.

Bucket List. Dir. Rob Reiner. Warner Brothers, Burbank, California, 2007. Movie.

Dirty Harry. Dir. Don Siegel. Malpaso Productions, Burbank, California, 1971. Movie.

Midnight in Paris. Dir. Woody Allen. Sony Picture Classics, Hollywood, Los Angeles, California, 2011. Movie.

Star Wars. Dir. George Lucas. Lucasfilm, San Rafael, California, 1999. Movie.

"The Baby Lab." Lesley Stahl. *60 Minutes*. CBS, New York, 12 November 2012. Television.

The Times They Are a-Changing. Bob Dylan. Columbia Studios, New York City, 1963. Studio Album.

About the Author

Jaellayna Palmer lives in Ayr, Ontario. She moved to Canada with her husband John (he is from New Zealand) in 1994 after serving for 8 years as volunteers at the Bahá'í World Centre in Haifa, Israel.

Originally from the US, she has a B.A. from Michigan State University and an MSc. from University of Surrey (UK). Currently self-employed, she helps clients design and deliver educational materials with an emphasis on inclusive teaching and learning strategies.

As she transitions to retirement, she plans to do more writing, increase her work as a volunteer for the Climate Reality Project, and continue exploring the world. She is passionate about fitness, hiking, travel, music (especially big band and 60s rock), reading, and tap dancing.

Her professional writing includes working as a ghost writer for a book, being a freelance newspaper columnist, and developing educational materials for adult learners. Since early 2016 she has been a contributing author to the site http://www.bahaiteachings.org.

This is the first full-length book she has written under her own name.

For more information or links to samples of some of her other writing, please visit http://www.jaellayna.org.

About the Illustrator

Doug Schaefer, originally from Waterloo, Ontario, studied cartooning and illustrating at Sheridan College. Doug says "This was all before there were computers to make graphic design easy." But anyone who has seen his illustrations (including the ones in this book) know that there's nothing easy about creating such original and engaging artwork.

He works at the University of Guelph where his drawing, cartooning, digital photography, and other skills are a valued addition to Teaching Support Services and the Office of Open Learning.

Doug, his wife Mary Ruth, and their twin sons live in Orangeville, Ontario. His personal interests include karate, taking history classes, reading, and film classics. He and his family are presently between rough coat collies.